FIJIANS IN TRANSNATIONAL PENTECOSTAL NETWORKS

FIJIANS IN TRANSNATIONAL PENTECOSTAL NETWORKS

KAREN J. BRISON

Australian
National
University

ANU PRESS

MONOGRAPHS IN
ANTHROPOLOGY SERIES

Australian
National
University

ANU PRESS

Published by ANU Press
The Australian National University
Canberra ACT 2600, Australia
Email: anupress@anu.edu.au

Available to download for free at press.anu.edu.au

ISBN (print): 9781760465599
ISBN (online): 9781760465605

WorldCat (print): 1357136326
WorldCat (online): 1357136284

DOI: 10.22459/FTPN.2023

Cover design and layout by ANU Press. Cover photograph by Karen J. Brison.

This book is published under the aegis of the Anthropology in Pacific and Asian Studies editorial board of ANU Press.

Contents

Acknowledgements

The research was funded by National Science Foundation grant 1024201 and a grant from the Pentecostal and Charismatic Research Initiative, administered by the Center for Civic and Religious Culture, University of Southern California, and funded by the John Templeton Foundation. I thank Donald E. Miller, Richard Flory and the other staff members of the Center for Civic and Religious Culture for their support and for organising two very stimulating workshops for the scholars working under the Pentecostal and Charismatic Research Initiative. I thank Stacey Jackson and Meaghan Jain for help with research in Fiji. I am grateful to Robert Samet for his close reading of the manuscript and for astute suggestions for revising the introduction. I thank Matt Tomlinson for his help and support as series editor and the two anonymous reviewers for their helpful suggestions. Above all, I thank members of the Harvest Ministry and other friends in Suva for their generosity in taking care of me and helping me to understand their world.

Portions of Chapter 5 have appeared as 'Becoming Blessed: Happiness and Faith in Pentecostal Discourse' in *The Routledge Handbook of Language and Emotion*, edited by Sonya Pritzker, Janina Fenigsen and James Wilce (Milton Park: Routledge, 381–94).

1

Introduction

My first encounter with the Harvest Ministry, an independent Fijian Pentecostal church, was in April 2005, when a friend invited me to attend the Sunday morning service with her at the main church in Suva.[1] As we entered the large circular auditorium with stadium-style seating, I looked up curiously at the hundred or more flags of nations around the world hanging from the ceiling. This Sunday, the church was packed with more than 1,000 people because the Harvest Ministry was having its monthly 'combined service' where those who usually attended the separate Fijian, Hindi and English language services designed to serve Fiji's major ethnic groups came together for one English service. The service began with announcements for upcoming events, such as the weekly youth service that afternoon, Wednesday night 'cell' (prayer) group meetings, and a special workshop to be hosted by American guests Kenneth and Gloria Copeland in the next month. Pastor Anare, an indigenous Fijian man who looked to be in his late 30s, took the floor and told us that next Sunday was 'Million Soul Sunday'. The Harvest Ministry would join with churches around the world to win 1 million souls for God in the next 10 years. 'We believe,' he said, 'it is possible if we, as a body of Christ around the world, come together in unity and combine our resources together, it is possible to win the entire world for God.' He reminded the congregation that they should continue their prayers on Monday, because Monday in Fiji would be Sunday in the many

---

1   In accordance with Internal Review Board protocols at Union College, I have used a pseudonym for the Harvest Ministry and I have also used pseudonyms for all the individuals mentioned in the book. I have changed names and some biographical details to protect the identities of my interlocutors.

nations on the other side of the dateline and it was important for everyone in the world to pray together. 'I want you to look up because the world is in [this church],' he said, pointing to the flags hanging from the ceiling:

> I want you to look up and look at one of the flags of the world ...
> And as you pray, focus on that one particular nation. I believe that if
> all of us focus on one flag we will be praying for the whole world and
> this particular initiative of reaching 1 million souls for God, amen?

Pastor Anare then turned to the call for tithes and offerings, reminding the congregation that their debts had been cancelled by Jesus's death and that now they should give to God the tithe of 10 per cent of their income owing to Him and should then add more money to demonstrate faith and obedience. Those who gave generously would receive the prosperity and health that God intended for his people:

> The Bible says give generously and do so without a grudging heart
> and because of this the Lord your God shall bless you in all your
> work and everything you put your hand to.

He explained that possessions could only transform individual lives if given away:

> We are able to overcome as Christians and believers. We are able to
> overcome because of the power of the blood of Jesus Christ that he
> shed, amen? Listen, that blood had no power unless it was given,
> amen? If Jesus had not given that blood sacrificially, it wouldn't
> have had any power. But because he was willing to give that blood
> sacrificially for your sin and my sin, it has enormous power. That
> is the power of giving. Giving has the power to overcome ... And,
> friends, also when we give it has the power to overcome every force
> of poverty, selfishness, self-centredness and greed, hallelujah! Your
> gift has the power to overcome, amen? [To overcome] the spirit of
> poverty, the spirit of greed and self-centredness.[2]

After the tithes and offerings were collected and duly blessed, Pastor Anare asked the congregation to give a warm welcome to 'the Father of the House', the senior and founding pastor, Pastor Vili, who had just returned from a trip to visit Harvest Ministry missionaries from Fiji and Papua New Guinea serving in Tanzania. Pastor Vili, a tall indigenous Fijian man in his mid-40s, told us he had started his trip by speaking at The Lighthouse, a 7,000-member

---

2   This and other sermons were recorded and transcribed by the author.

church with an American pastor in Nairobi. This had reminded him of a trip to The Lighthouse in Nairobi six years earlier when the Lord had 'spoken to him' about opening up Africa to the Harvest Ministry:

> I remember when I stepped on that stage six years ago, Acts 1:8 became so real to me. I asked the people, 'How many of you know where Fiji is?' Just a few people raised up their hands. Later on I found out that they were from New Zealand … Then I said, 'Well how many of you know a part where Fiji is written in the Bible?' No one raised up their hand. I mentioned Acts 1:8 and I said, 'If you really want to see where Fiji is, it is in Acts 1:8. Jesus said, "When the power of the Holy Spirit comes upon you, you shall be my witness first in Jerusalem, Judea, Samaria and then all the other parts of the earth." The farthest-most place from where Jesus uttered those words in Jerusalem is the tiny nation in the Pacific Ocean of Fiji. And it was there in Kenya when the Lord spoke to me in that meeting where He said, 'I really believe that Fiji … has a very special place in the heart of God regarding the fulfilment of the Great Commission.' So I came back with that word that the Lord placed in my heart and it was on that journey that I said, 'We have to build a bridge from Fiji to Africa to Asia to Europe and other parts of the world.'

I was intrigued by Pastor Vili's neat reversal of the Great Commission's call for Christians to take the gospel to the 'ends of the earth', a message that once inspired Euro-American Christians to send missionaries to Africa, Asia and the Pacific. Pastor Vili suggested that those 'at the ends of the earth', like Fiji, now had a special call to spread the gospel. As Pastor Vili continued, he noted that Fiji had a long history of sending missionaries to other areas of the Pacific; indeed, Fijians working with the London Missionary Society had been among the first to bring Christianity to Papua New Guinea in the nineteenth century in missions that were referred to as the 'Deep-Sea Canoe' (Garrett 1982; Tippett 2014). But as Acts 1:8 proclaimed, God wanted people to spread the gospel to the ends of the earth, not just to their neighbours. Pastor Vili continued:

> Because God's call is always a global call and as we study the mission history we see that [in] 200 years of Christianity in Fiji, you know, our forefathers started sending out missionaries to other parts of the Pacific and over the years we have discussed launching what they call the Deep-Sea Canoe and they have already launched the Deep-Sea Canoe. But the problem with the Deep-Sea Canoe, it's been launched from the Pacific and still remains in the Pacific and as I travel around the Pacific, I see that a lot of young people they have the passion to be of use to God.

Pacific churches lacked money to send missionaries, Pastor Vili continued, so he had worked for an international parachurch organisation, Every Home for Christ, that specialised in training and sending missionaries to fulfil the Great Commission in Matthew 28:16–20 to spread the gospel all over the world, particularly to what Every Home and other contemporary groups referred to as 'unreached people groups' who had 'not yet heard their first gospel'.[3] When Every Home for Christ transferred its regional headquarters out of Fiji, Pastor Vili founded his own church, in 1990, to employ the Fijians that he had recruited to work for Every Home. The Harvest Ministry then created its own streamlined training program for missionaries, which included an accreditation through an Oral Roberts University program at the Harvest Ministry Bible College. These efforts had come to fruition a few years before that 2005 sermon when Pastor Vili sent a handful of Fijian and Papua New Guinean missionaries to Tanzania. He described his recent visit to these missionaries and to a Tanzanian Pentecostal bishop (a term that is used loosely in many Pentecostal churches to refer to people who lead church networks) working with them, accentuating the gap between the Fijians and East Africans by joking about the hardships he had endured when the group had gone to visit some 'unreached peoples', the Maasai. During this trip they had slept on cow skins in mud huts, eaten cow hearts and drunk cow blood, which caused 'runny stomach'. They had also spent long hours in hot, dusty vans with no opportunity to wash for several days. Apparently, all were not equal in God's world. As I learned in later sermons, Harvest Ministry pastors saw themselves as leading the charge passed onto them by the British and the London Missionary Society so many decades before to bring both Christianity and civilisation to those still 'sitting in the back rows' (see also Ryle 2005, 2010).

My interest was already caught by these early parts of the service. I had regularly attended a Methodist church—some 60 per cent of indigenous Fijians are Methodist—in Rakiraki, a village on the north-east side of Viti Levu, the main island of Fiji, where I had conducted almost two years of research between 1997 and 2003. There had been a weekly collection, a monthly tithe paid by each lineage and a large annual village fundraising for the church, as well as special collections for particular causes like sending

---

3   'Unreached people groups' are defined by the Joshua Project (joshuaproject.net/definitions.php) as 'a people group among which there is no indigenous community of believing Christians with adequate numbers and resources to evangelize this people group'. The Harvest Ministry often referred to the Joshua Project and also spoke of 'unreached people groups' (as originally defined by the Joshua Project) as groups with less than 5 per cent Christian adherents.

the choir to the annual national choir competition in Suva. Requests for money were so common that people often grumbled about them. Like Pastor Anare, Methodist pastors had encouraged people to be less selfish and to think of others. But Methodist discourse linked humility and selfless service to the *vanua*, the hierarchical, landholding community that is the centre of indigenous Fijian culture and society. When people performed their duties (*i tavi*) and carried their burdens (*i colacola*), designated according to gender, age and rank in the *vanua*, they secured their place in Heaven and God blessed the community with abundant harvests. There was no talk of individual financial gain or of Fiji's mission to spread the gospel to the world.

The Methodist Church in Fiji was strongly associated with indigenous Fijian culture. Methodist missionaries had initially worked through high chiefs in south-eastern Fiji, resulting in a close association of indigenous Fijian chiefs and Christianity (Kaplan 1995). The Bible, hymnal and other Methodist literature were translated into Fijian in the nineteenth century and the leadership of the Fijian Methodist Church was entirely in the hands of Fijians. Methodist sermons were almost always in Fijian. The Methodist Church, although conceptually distinct from the clan and lineage structure, also reinforced the *vanua* with local chiefs and lineage elders sitting at the front of the church and often serving as lay preachers (*dau vunau*) leading services. Men sat on one side of the church in order of seniority with women on the other side with older and more senior women in front. Methodist sermons frequently reminded people of the importance of conforming to Fijian tradition through respectful dress and comportment and playing one's role in the community (Brison 2007a; see also Ryle 2010; Tomlinson 2009).[4]

The Harvest Ministry challenged the close association between church, indigenous Fijian identity and the *vanua*. In the main Suva church, the auditorium was circular, and people sat in nuclear family groups so there was no obvious ranking by gender and age. Pastors were referred to by their first names and even nicknames, flouting the indigenous Fijian practice of avoiding the first names of senior people as a sign of respect. In addition to the weekly Fijian service, there was an English service every week and there were also weekly Hindi services to include members of the Indo-Fijian descendants of late nineteenth and early twentieth–century indentured servants brought by the British to work in sugar plantations, who constitute

---

4   Tomlinson (2009) and Brison (2007a) both note that indigenous Fijians distinguish *lotu* (church) from *vanua* (ranked community), but that there is considerable overlap between the two.

about a third of Fiji's population.[5] The Methodist Church emphasised lineages and reminded people of their duty to uphold the *vanua* and to restore Fijian society to an original perfect state established when chiefs led the conversion to Christianity where people had observed custom and played their designated roles (Tomlinson 2009). In contrast, the Harvest Ministry called on individuals to transform their lives, to overcome poverty, and to support their senior pastor's novel vision of Fijian missionaries leaving the Pacific and going to other areas of the world. Pastors Anare and Vili also encouraged people to think of themselves as important contributors to the world community. I wondered what the appeal of this vision was for the Fijians who attended the church and supported its overseas endeavours through their tithes and offerings.

The Harvest Ministry vision of Fijians bringing civilisation and Christianity to a world community was cast in different language nine years later, during a Sunday service in July 2014 that I attended after I had been studying the church for several years. The years between the 2005 service and the 2014 service had been turbulent ones in Fiji. Army Commodore Voreqe ('Frank') Bainimarama took over the government in a coup in 2006 and introduced measures to erode the position of indigenous Fijian chiefs and the Methodist Church that supported them. Bainimarama's government also challenged Fiji's political and economic ethnic pluralism that was entrenched through such things as 'racial voting', which designated a fixed number of seats for Indo- and indigenous Fijians, and a small number of seats to represent Fijians from other ethnic groups, with each community voting for its own slate of candidates. International sanctions that followed the coup had disrupted the economy. These political and economic conditions had led many Fijians to migrate to Australia, New Zealand and other areas, and had prompted those at home to emphasise their professional ties to the outside world, perhaps in order to pave the way for migration in the future or as an attempt to distance themselves from chiefly leadership.[6]

---

5   The Methodist Church of Fiji and Rotuma also has a division for Indo-Fijians, although there are very few Indo-Fijian Methodists—only about 2,250 out of a total church membership of over 225,000 (see worldmethodistcouncil.org/member-churches/name/fiji-and-rotuma-methodist-church/). The Methodist Church does not bring Indo-Fijians and indigenous Fijians together for common services.

6   Newland (2012) and Tomlinson (2013) both noted the attempts of some Fijians to distance themselves from the Methodist Church in the period when Bainimarama was criticising the Methodist Church for opposing his regime.

This Sunday, the service began with a mystifying combination of management-speak, fundraising and religion. Pastor Vili encouraged church members to buy shares of 1,000 FJD (about 500 USD) in the church's new project, the Global Development Corporation, which sounded at first like a modest business venture. The project would begin with a small shopping plaza and then add a cement factory, a hotel and a consulting firm to give church members advice on developing plans for their own businesses. But Pastor Vili went on to show that this modest beginning was part of a much larger vision. He assured the congregation that the world was 'tipping' towards Fiji. Although Fiji was a tiny island nation, the Harvest Ministry was at the forefront of God's plan to spread the gospel to all areas of the world and had missionaries everywhere. Pastor Vili said that he and the elders who founded the church had a vision, that they institutionalised this vision in the church and that the church now channelled God's anointing to Fiji. Those who submitted to their anointed men of God and 'sowed seeds' by buying shares in the Global Development Corporation would share in the prosperity. The church was unique among Fijian enterprises, he continued, in being a global institution with missionaries in 'unreached people groups' around the world. The Fijian missionaries would bring the 'two hands of the gospel'—that is, salvation from the Lord and help in developing small businesses and good work habits—to these neglected and lost people. When they experienced improvement in their standard of living, they would provide a market for Fijian goods. Pastor Vili concluded by pointing out that he could have left Fiji and taken a good job with Every Home for Christ, but he wanted to stay home to help those who had worked with him from the beginning and to help Fiji to become a blessing to the world.

The Harvest Ministry, Moral Transformation and Fijian Middle-Class Projects

In the following pages, I look first at the appeal of the Harvest Ministry, and the world community it envisions, to Fijians and then examine the ways this imagined community is realised in practice through following Fijian and Papua New Guinean missionaries to East Africa and to Papua New Guinea. Pentecostalism is known for spreading Euro-American individual-centred moral systems and possibly paving the way for free market economies, processes that seem to be evident in Pastor Vili's emphasis on progress, individual initiative and Fijians conveying business-sense and development to East Africans. Pentecostalism is also known for imagining a flat transnational community where those on the periphery participate as equals to those from the centre, possibly paving the way for new ideologies from the global south that challenge entrenched world inequalities. The importance of this vision is apparent in Pastor Anare and Pastor Vili's suggestions that Fijians are at the forefront of a world Christian movement. As I examine the Harvest Ministry in Fiji, East Africa and Papua New Guinea, I suggest that understanding Pentecostalism as a global force requires close ethnographic examination of particular contexts. Pentecostalism neither spreads Euro-American moral and economic systems nor leads to a systematic critique of these ideas. Instead, the moral and economic impact of Pentecostalism is shaped everywhere by the way it is incorporated into local projects.

Turning first to the appeal of the Harvest Ministry to Fijians, I argue that the Harvest Ministry is one of several middle-class projects in contemporary Fiji through which a growing group of urban, professional indigenous Fijians create new leadership roles and new kinds of communities. The Harvest Ministry draws on common Pentecostal themes, such as the importance of individual agency and participation in a world Pentecostal community that transcends local cultural differences. But the ways that these themes are realised in the local context is shaped by the particular project of creating new roles and communities for an urban, professional class. This class project stems from a series of changes in Fiji. Some of these, like those following on from the 2006 coup, are relatively recent. Others have been gradual trends over the past three or four decades that have increased the number of indigenous Fijians, and particularly those who do not come from high-ranking families, with good professional jobs in urban areas. These changes include the removal of colonial restrictions on commoner Fijians moving to urban areas, and affirmative action policies of the 1980s and 1990s directed at increasing the educational attainments of indigenous Fijians, particularly those of non-chiefly status (Ratuva 2013, 173).

The expanding group of indigenous Fijians in good professional jobs is interested in creating new leadership roles that highlight achieved success and communities that relax some of the many protocols structuring *vanua* life, some of which they see as antithetical to professional success. In rural *vanua*, successful younger siblings with careers overseas or in Suva are respected and their money is coveted for village causes. But they are often spoken of as the 'children of the workplace' (Brison 2003, 2007a), submitting to elders in the village who are in charge of the *vanua* and who take a good part of the credit for the money that affluent urban siblings contribute to their lineages for funerals and other events. *Vanua* life requires respect (*veidokai*) for elders and village traditions, which involves displaying shame (*madua*) in front of those of higher rank. People must be willing to give time and resources to communal work and to put aside personal plans to spend many hours drinking kava and socialising to show respect for others (Erasaari 2013). Many Fijians view these qualities as antithetical to those required to succeed in professional jobs where people have to manage their time and resources, deal with new situations and present an impressive persona (Williksen-Bakker 2002). Rural chiefs are also constrained by many social obligations to the extent that, in some areas of Fiji, it is difficult to find people willing to serve in these positions (Erasaari 2013).

Urban professional indigenous Fijians also differ from previous generations in aspiring to a cosmopolitan identity in the wake of a series of coups since 1987 that led to economic downturns. The combined political and economic instability prompted people to keep options for outmigration open for themselves and their children through such measures as sending their children to multi-ethnic schools to improve their English (Brison 2014). Further, when Army Commodore Frank Bainimarama staged a coup in 2006, he began a series of measures to erode the privileged place of chiefs, such as reforming land rent policies that had given them a disproportionate share of rent monies for leased land and abolishing the Great Council of Chiefs through which they influenced government policy. These measures made chiefly-style leadership less attractive. Many members of the indigenous Fijian urban professional community, particularly those employed in government and in government-controlled parts of the finance industry, also came under attack for corruption and disloyalty (Ratuva 2013, 173). In 2010, Bainimarama banned the annual conference of the Methodist Church, an event that often highlights chiefs, for several years. These measures all prompted some people to distance themselves from chiefly leadership and the Methodist Church.[7]

All of these political and economic changes have led to a series of middle-class projects through which successful urban professionals seek ways to establish new leadership roles that emphasise their ties to the external world over their position within the *vanua*.

---

7   Although the Harvest Ministry supported the regime deposed by Bainimarama, the head pastor also counselled church members not to oppose the government and many church leaders were proud of the fact that their annual convention was allowed in years other church conventions were banned.

Fijian middle-class projects share a generic resemblance with similar attempts to construct new leadership roles for urban professionals in other areas of the global south where affluent professionals try to distinguish themselves from traditional elites by emphasising their good education, ability to consume mass-produced goods and facility with the outside world (see, for example, Besnier 2009 on neighbouring Tonga; Dickey 2016 on India; Gewertz and Errington 1999 on Papua New Guinea; Liechty 2003 on Nepal). However, as Dickey (2016), Ortner (2003), Liechty (2003) and others argue, social class is not a unitary phenomenon but is realised as numerous class projects fashioned when individuals attempt to convert access to economic resources into social and cultural capital (Bourdieu 1986). Consequently, ways of constructing class-based identities will differ from place to place, since the social and symbolic systems within which individuals manoeuvre are locally specific.

In Fiji, for instance, a history of ethnic pluralism makes it much more likely that Indo-Fijians will work in private businesses while indigenous Fijians are clustered in government bureaucracies and in jobs at banks and insurance agencies. This economic pluralism limits the degree to which emerging middle-class identities cross ethnic divisions since Indo- and indigenous Fijians tend to work in different places and have different experiences. In contrast, in Papua New Guinea a very small number of successful people from a wide variety of ethnic groups cluster in the same kinds of jobs and interact frequently, so middle-class projects cross ethnic lines (Gewertz and Errington 1999). There may also be more than one middle-class project in a given society, leading to different kinds of class-linked identities. In Fiji, some successful indigenous urban professionals join Pentecostal churches while others emulate the 'part-European' elites of colonial days through de-emphasising local cultural identities and emphasising facility in transnational fashion, technology and so on. Still others find communities of successful professionals and new kinds of identities by spending time with the 'old boys' clubs of elite, secondary schools.

In Fiji, Pentecostal churches like the Harvest Ministry are often part of indigenous Fijian middle-class projects because they allow for some renegotiation of social roles reinforced by the Methodist Church. The Harvest Ministry, for instance, as apparent in the services described above, implicitly challenged the ranking by age and gender in the *vanua* reinforced by the Methodist Church. Instead, the Harvest Ministry drew attention to professional achievements through such means as portraying church leaders as business experts who would bring prosperity to Fiji and to the world through the Global Development Corporation. Services also often emphasised that Pastor Vili, and other senior church leaders, had been successful in professional careers before joining the church. This kind of rhetoric helped to validate achieved success in business, something that many Fijians felt violated the obligations of chiefs to care for their community instead of pursuing personal profit (Pauwels 2020; White 2015). These constructions also legitimated behaviours and styles that defied *vanua* protocol, such as the ability to 'sell oneself' by portraying Fijians as equal participants in world Pentecostal and business arenas. The church, as was also evident in the services described above, located its members in a world community in which church leaders were shown to be successful participants who could do things like bring the gospel to the ends of the earth and establish a corporation that would build a global market for Fijian goods. Such messages implicitly contrasted church leaders—successful participants in a world community—with *vanua* elders who had a distinctly local kind of power.

Through joining the Harvest Ministry and other Pentecostal churches, people gained some independence from the *vanua* since they were forbidden by the church from participating in the frequent kava ceremonies that reinforced and acknowledged the *vanua* hierarchy. The Harvest Ministry, like many Pentecostal churches, provided a moral justification for achieved success by linking such success to good habits and to God's favour (see also Gewertz and Errington 1999). This helped affluent urbanites to fend off at least some of the requests from less prosperous relatives, although most people continued to give money to relatives and to the *vanua*. When enlisted for *vanua* causes they did not support, people could excuse themselves in morally acceptable terms by saying that they were Pentecostals who needed to give money to church causes. In doing so, they both became respected church elders and avoided alienating their kin. Church members also supplemented their kin and *vanua* networks with new ones that brought them together with other successful people who could help each other with business contacts, finding jobs, getting their children into good schools and other things (see also Burdick 1993; Chesnut 1996; Gershon 2006; Gewertz and Errington 1999; Gooren 1999; Lindhardt 2009; Martin 2001; Maxwell 1998; Wiegele 2004).

The Harvest Ministry illustrated well the locally specific nature of middle-class projects and the ways Fijian projects cemented rather than challenged ethnic divisions and identities. To achieve greater recognition and autonomy for successful indigenous Fijians, Harvest Ministry pastors drew on, but reformulated, the model of the *vanua*. *Vanua* were attached to particular localities from which, in theory, the ancestors or *vu* of the group had first emerged on earth. In the *vanua*, each person nurtured and cared for others (*veilomani*), respected and obeyed those of higher rank (*veidokai*) and gave service to others and support to the community (*veiqaravi*) (Toren 2004, 2006, 2007, 2011). The mutual service of community members was in some contexts translated as a form of tribute to the chief (*i liuliu* or *tui*), who would channel spiritual efficacy (*mana*) to the community (Toren 1999). In the Harvest Ministry, church members were directed to care for one another, but also to direct their love to the less fortunate peoples of the world. Church members also both preserved the community through reciprocal performance of duties (*i tavi*) and directed tribute, in the form of tithes and offerings, to the senior pastor. Particularly in the period following the Bainimarama coup, pastors cast these ideas in a language of free enterprise, speaking of the importance of a strong corporate church structure, where the head pastor ensured 'brand' consistency and channelled anointing to the church. Once properly branded, the 'productivity' of the church could be exported and 'reproduced' elsewhere.

Through this rhetoric, successful urban professionals could define a status for themselves that was similar, but superior, to that of rural elders, by showing that they could go beyond the local agency of traditional chiefs by performing service (*veiqaravi*) and dispensing compassion (*veilomani*) in a world Christian community conversant in transnational business—a construction that became all the more attractive after the 2006 coup led people to want to emphasise facility with and ties to the outside world. Harvest Ministry rhetoric, in short, partially challenged the Fijian status quo by highlighting the leadership of urban indigenous Fijians, but, as I will outline below, it offered no serious challenge to ethnic divisions, the importance of indigenous Fijian culture or the position of senior men in a hierarchical community (see also Morgain 2015).

In other ways, the Harvest Ministry created the possibility for a more radical reimagining of inequality in Fiji by suggesting a movement away from reciprocal exchange between chiefs and commoners (Toren 1999, 2004) towards harder class divisions, in which wealth was seen as resulting from moral action and individual initiative, and giving was unilateral in the form of philanthropy (Cox 2018; Dickey 2016). While chiefs and followers were linked through personal ties and wide-ranging mutual obligations, Harvest Ministry philanthropy raised the status of the giver without any implication that his or her success was due to support from the recipients of these gifts. Moreover, church leaders encouraged wealthy businessmen to see themselves as similar to the colonisers of the past, ready to pass on the benefits of wealth and civilisation to the poor within their country and abroad (see also O'Neill 2010), thus implicitly placing the rising Christian indigenous middle class as part of transnational elite.

Pentecostalism as a Series of Local Projects

My broader point is that Pentecostalism, known for its consistent culture, common themes and practices, and emphasis on flat transnational networks, is everywhere used to address local concerns, and so has very different social and moral impacts wherever it is found.

Pentecostalism, like social class, is, in short, shaped by local projects. Pentecostalism, as Robbins (2007, 2009) and others have noted, has very similar rituals, practices and themes all over the world. For instance, Pentecostal churches everywhere encourage 'rupture' with past practices and beliefs and emphasise the importance of individual experience of God. Pentecostal churches also promote greater individualism by encouraging people to ignore traditions and communal constraints to make their own choice to receive God and by locating salvation in the 'interior self' (Robbins 2004a, 2004b; Robbins, Schieffelin and Vilaça 2014). This strong and consistent Pentecostal culture raises similar moral and social issues wherever Pentecostalism spreads, particularly when it promotes individualism in so-called sociocentric or communal cultures where individuals are thought to be defined by, and should in turn subordinate individual desires to, webs of relationships (Robbins 2004a, 2004b, 2007). These beliefs may pave the way for modern free market economic systems by promoting self-discipline and may support social class by eroding customary obligations to redistribute individual wealth. Pentecostal churches also often portray themselves as being participants in flat transnational networks, where people from the global south participate as equals, and where everyone leaves behind local cultural practices and identities to participate in God's 'kingdom culture' (for example, Coleman 2013; Englund 2003; Marshall-Fratani 1998; Vasquez and Marquardt 2003).

Examining particular churches like the Harvest Ministry, however, reveals that Pentecostal ideas and practices can have very different social and moral impacts depending on the ways these transnational ideas are used by individuals to solve the particular problems of their lives (see also

Daswani 2015; Macdonald and Falck 2020; Mangowan and Schwarz 2016, 4–5; McDougall 2020). A lively debate among Pacific Island scholars (for example, Robbins 2007 versus Mosko 2010) queries whether or not Christianity is indigenised by being interpreted in light of local beliefs. This debate overlooks the fact that people always draw on both local and Christian beliefs in the process of addressing particular life situations, so beliefs take on meaning in the context in which they are used. For example, while Pentecostalism generally emphasises the importance of individuals resisting social pressures to choose for themselves, the way that this individual choice is conceptualised can differ significantly according to the everyday concerns of believers. Individuals in some areas may freely choose to take control of their lives by cutting ties with kin and resisting traditional exchanges. Well-educated women in urban Mozambique, for instance, sometimes join Pentecostal churches to free themselves from obligations to less prosperous rural kin (van de Kamp 2016b). But in other places, people freely choose to join the same Pentecostal church as family members to keep peace in the family, as Ikeuchi (2019) argues is common among Brazilian Pentecostals in Japan who want to keep family together in the face of an inhospitable environment. In other situations, individuals may freely choose to submit to, and be moulded by, a senior pastor in order to establish their own authority through placing themselves within a lineage of belief, as Reinhardt (2014, 2015) says occurs in The Lighthouse in Ghana. All of these constructions highlight individual agency but have rather different effects on social relations.[8]

Likewise, as Coleman (2013) and others point out, the imagined transnational Pentecostal network is experienced in different ways across the world (see also Brison 2017b). For example, the Swedish Word of Life Church and the Nigerian Redeemed Christian Church of God speak in similar terms of a decentralised world network of Christians. But the Swedish Word of Life Church has the resources necessary to send missionaries to

---

8   Finally, individualism (like sociocentrism or dividualism) is defined and enacted differently across cultures and contexts, and Pentecostalism encourages only some kinds of individualism. Individualism can be a lived practice, an experience of self or a value system (Boddy 1998; Lambek 2015; LiPuma 1998). Individualism also has various components, which do not always go together, and can be realised either as ideology or as lived practice (Robbins, Schieffelin and Vilaça 2014, 561). Individualism can mean that an interior self, integrated and bounded with a consistent character, is the locus of morality and decision-making (Becker 1995; Robbins 2004a), or it can mean freeing the mind from pressures of the body (Keane 2006, 2007). These beliefs oppose ideas that individuals are 'permeable' or 'porous', that is, shaped by the thoughts and emotions of others (Pype 2011), or 'dividual', the nexus of a set of relationships, each independently shaping discrete aspects of the person so that he or she is neither bounded nor internally coherent (Mosko 2010; Strathern 1990; Toren 2004, 2011).

Eastern Europe where, as Europeans from a wealthy nation, they have built some local following. The Redeemed Christian Church of God, on the other hand, has branches in many areas of Europe, but primarily attracts Nigerians and other Africans living in diaspora and has little outreach to the surrounding population (Coleman 2013). In Zambia, in contrast, people belong mostly to local church communities and look to pastors to connect them to the resources of a larger world (Haynes 2009, 2017; see also Corten and Marshall-Fratani 2001; Englund 2003; Marshall-Fratani 1998).

In the Harvest Ministry, as I will explain below and in subsequent chapters, pastors portrayed individual agency and submission to authority as compatible and encouraged people to become part of a hierarchical church community where pastors and other church leaders provided the links with a transnational world. Harvest Ministry pastors encouraged people to believe that they could freely choose to be born again and to accept Jesus into their lives. But 'going deeper' to realise one's purpose in God's world involved submitting to God, which in turn involved submitting to pastors who said that only they had the higher vision necessary to perceive God's plan. In this construction, individuals freely chose to submit to God and pastors (Brison 2017a; see also Daswani 2015; Reinhardt 2014, 2015). This particular configuration of individual agency and submission to community and authority made sense when viewed in the context of pastors' desire to build new kinds of leadership roles for urban indigenous Fijians, and the desire of many of the congregation members to attach themselves to the vision of a leader with knowledge of, and connections with, the outside world who would allow the organisation to accomplish things that would have been out of reach of ordinary Fijians (see also Haynes 2017). In this formulation, it was principally leaders who participated in transnational networks, while ordinary congregation members indirectly benefited from their leaders' connections. Similarly, the emphasis on membership in a world community and facility with a language of management was not a movement away from Fijian culture or national identity. Instead, emphasising the transnational connections of church leaders was part of an attempt to build new indigenous Fijian leadership roles by portraying urban professionals as superior to rural chiefs because urban professionals could participate as equals in a world community. The church's lack of interest in more general moral transformation towards greater individualism, or new kinds of identities as world citizens, was evident in the fact that ordinary members of the congregation sometimes joined the church because they were attracted to a message of individual empowerment and then left when they realised they were expected to submit to pastors and church leaders in the same way as they submitted to *vanua* elders.

Similarly, when I examined connections between Fijians and their partners in Papua New Guinea and East Africa, I found that the tendency of Pentecostalism to be pulled into local projects worked against the possibility of Pentecostalism creating a world community that superseded local identities. Church leaders and scholars of religion suggest a special connection between Christians in the global south that could produce challenges to entrenched world inequalities (for example, Anderson 2013; Jenkins 2006; Nazir-Ali 2009[9]). But in each of the nations involved in the Harvest Ministry network, church leaders highlighted the special qualities of their nation in an effort to redefine their own position in local society as people who were important in the outside world.

The result was an imaginary of the world community that endorsed Euro-American racial hierarchies and nineteenth-century social evolutionary theories. The new imaginary, however, highlighted the way that the particular characteristics of individual nations from the global south made them ideal to take on a civilising mission passed onto them from former colonial powers. In Fiji, pastors praised the abilities of indigenous Fijians to put community over self and to submit to leaders as key to their ability to bring blessings to Fiji and to the rest of the world. These constructions drew on nineteenth-century British colonial thinking where colonial officials working with chiefs from the south and east of Fiji suggested that indigenous Fijians were innately 'civilisable' because of their hierarchical chieftainships, and that Fijians from the south and east, where there were larger regional chieftainships, were more advanced in social evolution than those from the interior and west of the country (Kaplan 1995). Drawing on this rhetoric appealed to indigenous Fijian pride and also reinforced the position of successful indigenous Fijian male professionals, many of them from the south and east of Fiji, by linking their traditional authority within Fiji to an international language of business and Pentecostalism that suggested that the same characteristics that made them good Fijians also made them good businessmen and players in a world Christian community.

---

9   Nazir-Ali (2009), writing about the Anglican Church, suggests that Christianity is most effectively spread through local churches that will interpret Biblical messages in ways relevant to local life. He suggests, however, that too much localisation can cause problems in creating a cohesive transnational church.

Papua New Guineans, in contrast, emphasised the perceived strengths of Papua New Guineans as humble but tough people who had superior capacity to spread God's kingdom on earth; this was a construction that appealed to youth with blocked aspirations by suggesting paths to geographical mobility. Within Papua New Guinea, the church primarily involved people from coastal and island areas of Papua New Guinea missionising groups in the interior, a vision that endorsed previous colonial hierarchies. Finally, East Africans spoke of their capacities as networkers seeking to survive in the face of the curtailment of government jobs and services in the wake of structural adjustment and, perhaps realistically, perceived that self-help through 'mindset transformation', while distinctly limited, was the only option in a scarce environment. And they also endorsed earlier colonial schemes that placed agrarian groups above pastoral ones.

In short, indigenous Fijians, Papua New Guineans and East Africans were all looking for ways to formulate new leadership roles in local society by claiming facility with an outside world. This agenda caused them to focus on local uniqueness rather than on commonalities with others on the periphery of the world system. In the process, each group generally embraced colonial and postcolonial hierarchies rather than contesting them.

Orientations

The Harvest Ministry was founded in 1990 by Pastor Vili, who had left a career as a government engineer to work for an American parachurch organisation, Every Home for Christ. Before working for Every Home, Pastor Vili had served as a lay preacher (*dau vunau*) for the Methodist Church, as was the case for many successful Fijians. The Methodist Church relies heavily on lay preachers, as, in rural areas, there is only one ordained minister for a circuit of villages, which means that the minister appears in individual churches less than once a month. Many of the friends who Pastor Vili recruited to work with him had also served as Methodist lay preachers. When Every Home for Christ relocated its regional leadership outside of Fiji, Pastor Vili declined their offer to retain his position by moving, and instead decided to create his own church, partly to employ the many Fijians he had recruited to work for Every Home as missionaries in Fiji and Papua New Guinea.

In 2006, Pastor Vili, estimated that the church had about 50,000 members in Fiji (Newland 2010, 84). In practice, the size of the membership was hard to determine since many people attended for short periods and then left. At the monthly 'combined' service, the 3,000-seat main church in Suva was usually about 80–90 per cent full, giving a rough sense of the size of the membership. The Harvest Ministry also had smaller branches in Suva, in the other main cities of Fiji and in smaller towns. Outside of Fiji, membership fluctuated greatly; I encountered several tiny churches in Papua New Guinea, for instance, that people assured me had been much larger in the past when led by a more energetic and popular pastor. The Harvest Ministry also formed alliances with existing networks of churches when entering new countries and counted members of these churches as Harvest Ministry members. Therefore, international membership was subject to interpretation.

Harvest Ministry ideology was heavily influenced by Euro-American prosperity gospel preachers who attended the annual convention in Fiji, and who trained Pastor Vili. Such international superstars of prosperity theology as Ulf Ekman, Benny Hinn, Reinhard Bonnke and Myles Munro had spoken in Fiji, and Pastor Vili had spoken in Sweden at Ekman's Word of Life Church in Uppsala several times, and also had appeared in churches in the US and in other areas of the world, such as Latin America and Russia. As is typical of prosperity churches worldwide, pastors told the congregation that a tithe of 10 per cent of their income belonged to God, but that they should give beyond that 10 per cent as an act of worship. Congregation members were asked to give money for special projects, such as supporting missionaries, building a primary and then a secondary school, providing relief to victims of flooding, building churches in remote areas and supporting the development of a shopping plaza next to the church. Pastors doing the call for the offering often encouraged people to give sacrificially, beyond what was comfortably within their means, since only giving that caused hardship would truly show obedience to, and faith in, the Lord. As is typical in prosperity churches, pastors told stories of giving their last dollar only to find unexpected gifts of money shortly afterwards (see, for example, Harding 2000, 124).

The Harvest Ministry followed closely the model of prosperity churches in other areas of the world. The flags of other nations decorating the central church in Suva, symbolising its focus on world mission, were typical of Word of Faith churches in other nations. Like other Word of Faith churches, the Harvest Ministry emphasised world mission (Coleman 2000) and had missionaries in Papua New Guinea, other parts of the Pacific, East Africa, Cambodia, Europe and other areas. It was somewhat difficult to determine the number and location of Harvest Ministry missionaries at any one time since the church frequently moved people around and also included among their missionaries so-called 'tent-makers'—that is, people who had jobs overseas in institutions like the United Nations and volunteered to run small churches or prayer groups for the Harvest Ministry in the country where they worked. The Harvest Ministry also ran its own Bible college for its pastors in which it trained carefully selected recruits from East Africa, Papua New Guinea, Cambodia, Germany and other countries as well as Fijians. The ministry followed other Word of Faith churches in making extensive use of mass media. Services from the main church in Suva were broadcast on television and radio within Fiji and to congregations in the US, UK and Germany via the internet.

As Miller and Yamamori (2007) say is typical of independent Pentecostal churches, the Harvest Ministry combined a highly effective administrative structure with a clear and relevant message and well-staged services. Like many churches of its kind worldwide, the Harvest Ministry had large Sunday services, demonstrating the church's success and power, and small weekly cell group meetings where members could address personal issues and create a sense of an intimate community. Indeed, I was often impressed at the extent to which the large Harvest Ministry congregation felt like a small family church, with many core members having attended since the beginning and knowing each other personally.

While Harvest Ministry pastors and church members were dispersed widely across the Pacific, Europe, Asia and Africa, the pastors nevertheless formed a tight-knit community and knew each other well. Many of them had attended the same elite secondary boarding school, had been educated together at the ministry's Bible school, and came from the same regions of Fiji's second largest island, Vanua Levu, which was also Pastor Vili's home island. Pastors also saw each other frequently, communicated by phone or on Facebook, listened to each other's sermons over livestreaming, on DVD or in conventions in Suva and elsewhere, and delivered a common message using similar Bible verses and rhetorical devices. Pastors posted in different areas of the world met at the annual convention in Suva and also frequently visited each other. For instance, the leaders of a cell group that I joined in Suva visited missionaries in Cambodia and Tanzania several times during the time I knew them. The Harvest Ministry pastor in the UK and several of his congregation members visited the Fijian missionaries in Kenya over

Christmas four years in a row. I ran into Pastor Anare in Suva and the UK, and encountered Fijians posted in East Africa and Papua New Guinea both in those areas and in Suva.

Intrigued by questions about moral transformation and religious globalisation decentred from Euro-America, I studied the Harvest Ministry off and on for over 10 years, beginning at that service in 2005 but with most of the research conducted between 2010 and 2014. In Suva, I recorded and transcribed about 40 sermons. I joined a cell group and attended their weekly prayer meetings whenever I was in Suva, about nine months in total over a period of four years. I also became part of their church zone (a larger division consisting of several cell groups) for July and August 2010 and attended zone picnics, fundraisers and a get-together where we all performed songs and skits to break the ice and get to know each other better. I engaged in many conversations with people I met at the church who became my friends and also people who I knew from other contexts. I got to know more about the lives of several of my friends from church when they acted as hosts to undergraduates who I directed on terms abroad in Fiji. I also spent a year in 2011 and 2012 visiting Fijian and Papua New Guinean missionaries and their local partners in Kenya, Tanzania, Uganda and Madagascar, as well as in several areas of Papua New Guinea. In these areas, I stayed with Fijian missionaries and their families and their local affiliates for periods ranging from two to six weeks. I attended leadership training sessions, crusades, weekly church services and regional meetings. I travelled with Fijian and Papua New Guinean missionaries to visit so-called unreached people groups, and to visit friends including in a multinational community attached to the United Nations in Arusha, Tanzania. In August 2013, I attended a week-long retreat for members of the Harvest Ministry living in the UK. In these contexts, I observed and recorded about 30 sermons in weekly church meetings, leadership training sessions and crusades, as well as talking to Fijian and Papua New Guinean missionaries and their local affiliates about their lives and work with the church.[10]

---

10 Harvest Ministry pastors spoke in English when preaching to an audience of mixed nationality and ethnicity. In Suva, they also had Fijian-language services and often interspersed some Fijian in English services. Harvest Ministry church members sometimes spoke English with each other and sometimes spoke in various dialects of Fijian. They also interspersed Fijian words and phrases and kin terms in English sentences.

The Plan of the Book

Chapter 2 locates this study in a broader literature by examining two competing debates, one that stresses the capacity of Pentecostalism to spread Euro-American individualism and economic ideologies, and the other that views Pentecostalism as a potential vehicle through which Christians from the global south challenge Euro-American ideologies and the inequalities they support.

Chapters 3, 4 and 5 examine the Harvest Ministry as a church that appeals to successful urban indigenous Fijian professionals by creating new leadership roles and new kinds of communities that support professional careers and lifestyles. Part of the appeal of the urban church community involves an imaginary of the church's position as a vanguard spreading Christianity and economic development to the unreached of the world; consequently, these chapters move beyond Suva to show the ways in which Fijians imagine themselves to be spiritual guides in East Africa and Papua New Guinea. In Chapter 3, I compare concepts of religious agency as defined in the Harvest Ministry and in the Methodist Church, and more broadly compare the way church leadership is defined vis-a-vis the rural *vanua*. I also examine comparable notions of religious agency as expressed in the *sevusevu*—the ceremonial presentation of kava that marks all village events. Methodist sermons and *sevusevu* reinforce the *vanua* tracing religious agency, or blessings from God, to a community in proper order with each individual conforming to his or her traditional role based on age, gender and rank. Methodist sermons portray individuals as wilful, stubborn and selfish, and urge people to overcome these tendencies to contribute to community and conform to traditional ways. Harvest Ministry sermons appear to contest these ideas, encouraging people to leave traditional places and customs, forge forth in the world to play the role that God created for them in spreading his kingdom on earth, and to progress in their own lives and in the world community at large. But closer examination reveals that Fijian Pentecostals emphasise the importance of submitting to anointed men of God and playing one's role in an earthly church community, thus creating a *vanua* writ large, that is an orderly hierarchical community divorced from any particular place or culture that can be exported abroad. I locate these views within a historical progression from a reciprocal relationship between chiefs and members of the *vanua* to an increasingly hierarchical view of chiefly power fostered by the British. I suggest that the rhetoric of urban church leaders moves even further away from the idea that leaders have a reciprocal relationship with followers. The Harvest Ministry portrays leaders as providing sustenance and guidance to the less fortunate. As members of a professional class, these leaders neither depend on nor even necessarily know the less fortunate who they help through philanthropy, although, in some contexts, less wealthy church members provide spiritual labour in return for the material support of successful church leaders.

In Chapter 4, I suggest that this discourse suits successful urban professionals eager to carve a place for themselves at home and in a world community of Christians and of relatives living overseas. While many Fijians think that chiefs should not engage in business (Pauwels 2020; White 2015), church rhetoric provides alternative leadership roles that legitimate professional success. For instance, the church encourages successful people to see themselves as patrons who give money that then supports a great many less affluent church members, such as pastors, missionaries and church workers, who contribute spiritual labour in return. Many people experience the church community as meaningful and supportive and benefit from the contacts it establishes among affluent urbanities. But many others join the church expecting a greater emphasis on individualism and eventually leave when they realise that they are supposed to obey pastors and church elders. I suggest that the church works in a similar way for a small urban elite in Papua New Guinea.

In Chapter 5, I examine the way Harvest Ministry pastors draw parallels between Biblical stories of triumph over adversity and their personal lives to prompt people to see themselves as blessed. Pastors say that God has created each person to fulfil a particular role in spreading His kingdom. Misfortune results when people unwittingly pursue goals that are not part of God's plan for them, but people will ultimately find their place in God's kingdom and experience prosperity, happiness and good health. These messages help church members at home and abroad to see themselves as blessed, which in turn empowers them to face the challenges of racism and lack of family support overseas and to carve out new places for themselves in the urban Pacific.

Chapters 6, 7 and 8 focus on the Harvest Ministry's international networks to examine the extent to which a common critique of world inequality emerges in partnerships between churches in the global south. I argue that Fijians, Papua New Guineans and East Africans have significantly different views of the transnational Pentecostal community and that within each group leaders are primarily interested in redefining their own position in local society. These views prevent any common questioning of world inequality. Chapter 6 compares Fijian and Pacific Islander rhetoric about mission endeavours with those of European and North American organisations such as Every Home for Christ. Csordas (2009) and others suggest that religious flows from the global south may operate independently of economic and political global power structures and could lead to new ideas from the global south. Harvest Ministry conferences in Suva, on the other hand, adopt an older Euro-American view of unilinear development and see Fiji as spreading the benefits of Christianity and civilisation to unreached peoples who are isolated and neglected by their own co-nationals. They also draw on Euro-American imaginaries of childlike global southerners with natural faith who will revitalise spiritually cold people from the global north. Fijians see themselves as poised to help both those in the south and in the north, since, in their view, Fijians still have natural spirituality but long ago received the benefits of civilisation from the British. This view supports the position of a new Fijian Pentecostal middle class.

Chapters 7 and 8 examine Fijian and Papua New Guinean missionaries and their local partners in East Africa and Papua New Guinea. In Suva, sermons and conventions raised support from church members by portraying East Africans and Papua New Guineans as unreached peoples who knew nothing about the Bible and live in dire poverty. However, when Fijians and Papua New Guineans went overseas and to more remote areas of their own countries, they quickly realised that Christianity was widespread and that there were many organisations delivering various forms of international aid. This caused culture shock and forced missionaries to re-evaluate their assumptions. Chapter 7 begins with a small urban church in Port Moresby, capital of Papua New Guinea, that works with prosperous professional Papua New Guineans to transform the lives of youth in settlements through 'mindset transformation', offering paths to progress through 'faithfulness in small things' such as cleaning the church and participating in church choirs. Many young Papua New Guineans with limited employment prospects liked the idea that if they participated faithfully in the church, local businesspeople would sponsor them to go to Bible school in Fiji and on mission trips to other areas of the world. However, there was no special connection overall between Papua New Guineans and Fijians as fellow Christians from the global south. Many Papua New Guineans saw Fijians as 'culturally unable' to 'humble themselves' in ways necessary to successful mission work. In contrast, Papua New Guineans saw themselves as tough and used to living without money, enabling them to more effectively spread the gospel.

Each group drew on a set of ideas about the connection between 'simple village people' from the global south, which stemmed from Euro-American parachurch organisations, and interpreted them in ways that enhanced their own sense of distinctive cultural agency in a world community.

Chapter 8 turns to the Harvest Ministry in East Africa. Papua New Guinean and Fijian missionaries felt they were very different from East Africans. In the wake of structural adjustment, many educated East Africans looked to churches and non-governmental organisations as avenues to piece together networks of support, including international aid. Fijians and Papua New Guineans had not experienced the structural adjustment policies of international organisations such as the World Bank and International Monetary Fund and so had trouble understanding the conditions facing East Africans. Fijians were puzzled as to why East Africans were so poor despite what appeared to them to be abundant natural resources; they also perceived East Africans as having an inappropriate focus on money in matters of religion. Lacking extensive knowledge of world history and economic systems, pastors often concluded that Africans needed 'mindset transformation' and to learn good habits to prosper, views that were reinforced by many of the Euro-American religious groups with whom the missionaries interacted. However, working together over a period of years with neither side having a clear upper hand had led to a shared vision of a locally self-supporting church.

2

Pentecostalism and Global Moral and Economic Systems

In this chapter I examine debates about the capacity of Pentecostalism to effect transformation through forging distinctive transnational moral systems and economic ideologies. A robust literature examines the ways that Pentecostalism spreads Euro-American moral and economic systems by promoting modern, individuated selves and free market economies (for example, Cannell 2006; Keane 2007; Robbins 2004a, 2004b, 2007). At the same time, many scholars have noted that the fastest growing Pentecostal congregations are in the global south and that the major missionary-sending nations are now Brazil, Nigeria and South Korea. The growth of Pentecostalism and mission outside of Euro-America raises questions about the extent to which Pentecostalism is a vehicle for Euro-American moral and economic systems (Csordas 2009; van de Kamp and van Dijk 2010). Possibly a Pentecostalism emanating from the global south is producing new emphases and visions, perhaps even ones that contest hegemonic Euro-American moral and economic systems. Looking at specific churches such as the Harvest Ministry suggests that individuals everywhere are more likely to be concerned with local projects than global trends so that Pentecostal transformations occur through a series of local projects in which common themes may lead to different results.

Christianity, Individualism and Free Market Economies

A large literature links Christianity to the rise of the modern, self-monitoring, individuated self. Cannell (2006, 18–19), Keane (2006, 2007), Robbins (2004a, 2004b) and others argue that Christianity, particularly in its Protestant and Pentecostal forms, spreads Euro-American modernity through promoting the ideal of autonomous, individuated persons, unfettered by social relationships and conventions, whose agency lies in an interior self rather than in exchanges and relationships with others. Such beliefs have the potential to challenge moral and ontological systems where persons are believed to be relational or dividual—that is, constituted by exchanges with others and where relationships and communal traditions are considered more important than individual gain (for example, Robbins 2004a, 2004b, 2007; Ryle 2010; Strathern 1990). Eriksen, Blane and MacCarthy (2019), for instance, argue that a common theme of Pentecost is to extract individuals from extended family networks and rituals emphasising ancestral obligations in order to highlight the importance of nuclear family ties and an orientation towards the future.

In Fiji, Newland (2004, 2) suggests that Pentecostal churches are 'an avenue to reorder social life, diminishing the traditional social hierarchy in the process' and providing a way to struggle towards 'a modernity that is acceptable to village Fijians who are not rewarded by the chiefly system', such as women and young people. Ryle (2005, 2010), likewise, points to the potential of Pentecostal churches to empower individuals in contemporary Fiji by locating them within an international community and through stressing individual reciprocity with God over the specific reciprocal ties to the *vanua* emphasised in Methodism. Ernst (1996, 282–83, 2006), on the other hand, criticises Pentecostal churches for eroding communal ties. He suggests that, like Methodists in seventeenth-century England (Thompson 1966), contemporary Pacific Pentecostal churches promote social and political passivity by getting people to focus on individual salvation instead of enduring social inequalities. Through spreading 'Western' values emphasising individual achievement and initiative, Pentecostal churches may help individuals to marginally improve their own economic situation but are unlikely to lead to economic development in Third World nations of the twentieth and twenty-first centuries.

Extracting the individual from social conventions and networks and emphasising instead individual choice and self-monitoring may, in turn, be linked to free market economies. Comaroff and Comaroff (1991) argue that British nonconformist missionaries among the Tswana of South Africa in the nineteenth and early twentieth centuries taught ideas about time management, work, dress and a host of other daily habits conducive to producing a compliant workforce. A recent reformulation of this perspective argues that Pentecostalism promotes an empowered, self-disciplined, risk-taking and entrepreneurial self that is consistent with the demands for flexible, self-directed labour in post-Fordist capitalism and under neoliberal policies (for example, Brouwer, Gifford and Rose 1996; Heelas and Woodhead 2005).

The connection between religion, individualism and materialism is particularly striking in churches, like the Harvest Ministry, influenced by the prosperity gospel (also known as the gospel of health and wealth or the Word of Faith movement), a variety of Pentecostalism known for popularising the idea that God wants all believers to be 'healthy and wealthy'. Those who 'sow a seed'—that is, give money to the church—will tap into a global flow of 'anointing' and be blessed with material abundance (Bowler 2013; Coleman 2000). An early wave of analyses of the prosperity gospel saw it as strongly linked to neoliberalism and the impact of neoliberal policies on nations in the global south. Comaroff and Comaroff (2001, 2003) suggested that prosperity preaching was one of many types of 'occult economies' appealing to those on the margins of the world system. Those of the margins were increasingly exposed to, but cut off from achieving, lavish lifestyles. They also experienced precarity and lack of control in economies that were dominated by transnational capital as a result of neoliberal structural adjustment policies. Prosperity teachings also seemed to spread religious justification for a free market economy by 'valorizing both an individualised ethic of consumerism and a spirit of entrepreneurship' (summarised in Coleman 2011a, 28), and by suggesting that success in business was a sign of God's favour (Bowler 2013, 53; Brouwer, Gifford and Rose 1996; Hunt 2000; Newland 2004).

Ambitious theories about the link between Pentecostalism, Euro-American individualism and free market economies have, of course, been disputed on all fronts. Nuanced studies of particular Pentecostal churches show that religious beliefs may respond to conditions of life created by economic systems but cannot be reduced to ways of coping with those realities (Coleman 2011a). Prosperity churches appeal to many people for non-economic reasons: they create strong and supportive communities where even people of modest means can feel valued for their contributions (Harrison 2005; Premawardhana 2012; Wiegele 2004) and imbue people with a 'forward tilting' sense of 'expansive agency' that helps them to cope with adverse circumstances and to take risks (Coleman 2000; Haynes 2017; Luhrmann 2012; Piot 2010; Rial 2012). The 'charismatic gift', in which people give beyond their apparent capacity, is, for many believers, an act of faith that demonstrates confidence that God will provide and builds agency (Coleman 2006). Prosperity churches, as evident in the opening services, are not all about individual accumulation, since these churches encourage people to give their money and time to communal causes (Coleman 2006).

Moreover, neither Pentecostalism nor Christianity in general can 'be viewed as a singular project of individuality' (Coleman 2011b, 248). Pentecostalism encourages individuated selves in some ways by, for instance, stressing that individuals must choose to submit to Christ and by emphasising direct personal experience of God through prayer, healing and speaking in tongues. But Pentecostalism also encourages relational or 'dividuated' selves by emphasising that each person has an integral and unique place in the 'body of Christ' and in a real church community (for example, Brison 2017a; Daswani 2010, 444–46, 2015; Elisha 2011, 19; Morgain 2015; Mosko 2010; Schwarz 2010; Werbner 2011, 298).[1] Morgain (2015), for instance, argues that the Christian Mission Fellowship, a Fijian Pentecostal church, encourages individual decisions in some ways, but also emphasises the importance of playing a role in a church and world community, and submitting to church leadership. People may also stress relationships in some contexts and individual freedom of choice in other contexts (Coleman 2011b). Or they may focus on a particular kind of relationship, often with nuclear family, while trying to distance themselves from communal, lineage and extended family obligations linked to repaying ancestral debt

---

1   Christianity conceives of people at least in some contexts as dividuals immersed in communities, whose agency is defined contextually and through exchanges with humans as well as God (Mosko 2010, 2015; see Daswani 2010, 444–46, 2015; Werbner 2011, 298). People may, for instance, experience themselves as autonomous agents while participating in Pentecostal Church gatherings but continue to enact a more permeable or relational sense of self in everyday life (Chua 2012). Relational or porous selves are also found within the church. Pentecostals in Kinshasa, Congo, for instance, see ties with the Holy Spirit and church community as replacing the influence of ancestral blood ties (Pype 2011, 286–88, 298). There is a strong communal dimension to Pentecostalism. Christian selves 'born again' by receiving Jesus are generally immersed in both real church communities and an imagined world community of Christians (Coleman 2000; Elisha 2011, 10).

(Eriksen, Blane and MacCarthy 2019). Pentecostal churches are also often hierarchical and demand submission to church leaders (Bielo 2009; Brison 2017a; Daswani 2015, 63; Harrison 2005; Reinhardt 2014).[2]

In the following pages, I join a growing number of Pacific scholars in arguing that Pentecostalism generally reformulates ideas about both persons and community in ways that respond to local conditions, such that understanding the general impact of Pentecostalism requires looking at the variety of ways it is used in particular situations (for example, Macdonald and Falck 2020; McDougall 2020). As Barker (2012, 2014) notes, many areas of Melanesia are over 100 years, and two or three waves of different Christian churches, away from the first point of contact with Euro-American missionaries (and, indeed, many areas of the Pacific were first missionised by other Pacific Islanders). Often conversion from one variety of Christianity to another has more to do with power struggles within local communities than with grappling with Euro-American moral systems (Handman 2015). The significance of Pentecostal conversion may also address specific conditions created by the mainline churches they displace so that the moral transformation involved is locally specific, as appears to be the case in Fiji where, as I show in the next chapter, Pentecostal churches implicitly challenge the Fijian Methodist Church. Fer (2012), similarly, suggests that Youth with a Mission was appealing to many young Pacific Islanders because it was less puritanical than mainline churches dominant in many areas and seemed to celebrate local cultures through its emphasis on dance, even though affirming local cultures is not a general goal of Youth with a Mission.

The significance of Pentecostal beliefs and practices more generally lies in the ways they are used to address particular local concerns. Cox (2018), for example, argues that U-Vistract, a Ponzi scheme promoted through prosperity churches in Papua New Guinea, appealed to urban professionals by positioning them 'as Christian patrons, disbursing their resources generously and to good developmental effect', in contrast to corrupt national politicians appropriating dollars that were supposed to promote national development for personal gain. Many of the people Cox (2018) interviewed were not certain that they would get a lot of money by investing

---

2   A recent turn in the debate about Christianity and individualism has been to suggest that both Christianity and all societies include dividual, relational (or sociocentric) and individuated senses of the person, enacted as 'modalities' in response to different life problems (Daswani 2015), evoked as 'frames' for interaction (Schram 2015), or acting as different lenses for viewing aspects of the individual alternately serving as 'figure' and 'ground' (Lambek 2015).

in U-Vistract, but were dismayed at the current level of corruption in Papua New Guinea and were attracted by the prospect of being part of a 'reformed nation led by faithful Christian citizens'. Maggio (2015) similarly suggests that both adherents of prosperity churches and groups that identify with Judaism in the Solomon Islands are primarily concerned with opposing what they see as decades of unfulfilled promises due to government corruption. They seek to replace secular governments with a theocracy in which individuals directly answer calls from God (Maggio 2015, 320).

The apparently contradictory emphases on individual agency and submission to community evident in many Pentecostal churches make sense when viewed in the context of the 'issues of the world that people of the region have to confront day in and day out' (Mangowan and Schwarz 2016, 4–5). Mangowan and Schwarz (2016), for example, argue that a charismatic renewal movement among the Yolngu Aboriginal community of northern Australia both promotes individuated selves in prompting people to take responsibility for their lives to overcome addiction and other problems and encourages relational selves in drawing people together around kin experiencing problems. Hardin (2018), likewise, suggests that Samoans make use of the individuating strains of Pentecostalism to encourage people to resist communal pressures to eat and to take control of their diet in the face of high rates of type 2 diabetes. But Pentecostals avoid celebrating individual choice and instead say that they are following God's will because this construction allows them to focus on personal health in a way that does not contest the paramount importance of community over the individual.

Likewise, in Fiji, the particular construction that emphasised individuals choosing to subordinate themselves to a church community made sense when viewed in the context of successful urban professionals looking for new models of community and leadership in the wake of the economic and political changes that destabilised indigenous Fijian chiefly traditions of the past.

Decentred Religious Globalisation?

A second group of scholars point out that religious globalisation no longer exclusively or evenly primarily emanates from Europe and North America, suggesting the potential for religion to spread new visions from periphery to centre. In fact, a growing number of churches, most notably from Nigeria, Brazil and Korea, have spread to other areas of the global south, leaving open the possibility of new ideas about morality and society (for example, Coleman 2013; Coleman and Maier 2016; Freston 2001, 2005; Kim 2015; O'Neill 2010; Oosterbaan, van de Kamp and Bahia 2020; van de Kamp 2016a; van Wyk 2014). Csordas (2009, 3–4) argues that at first:

> The cultural influence of globalisation is unidirectional, from globalizing centre to passive periphery, with religion a neocolonial form of cultural imperialism … [But] once global channels are open, the flow of religious phenomena … is at least bi-directional, more likely multi-directional.

Migration, increased travel and increasingly accessible mass media have made it possible for religions to travel in many directions, as, for instance, when Australian, American and European tourists travel to Brazil and discover ayahuasca rituals, and when Brazilian migrants to the Netherlands and Portugal bring their rituals with them (Csordas 2009, 5–6).

Multi-directional religious globalisation from periphery to centre and from one area of the periphery to another is not new. Yoruba Orisha cults travelled with slaves from West Africa to the United States, the Caribbean and Brazil, and then travelled back and forth within these areas, across the Atlantic back to East Africa and from Sierra Leone to Nigeria as freed slaves moved from area to area (Cohen 2009; Malory 2009). Umbanda cults in Brazil that combined Catholicism and Orisha rituals then travelled to other areas of South America (Massonnier 2020) and to Europe and North America (Groisman 2009). Csordas (2009, 7, 9) also argues that there is now cross-fertilisation among indigenous religions producing a 'pan-indigenous' form of religion, as when the Hopi create a reggae society embracing a 'kindred Rastafarian spirituality'. Finally, re-globalisation of world religions from periphery to centre is increasingly common as migrants move to Europe and North America and take their own forms of Christianity and other world religions with them (Csordas 2009, 8).

A prime example of the way contemporary religious globalisation moves in many directions is the 'lusosphere' in which religions travel from Brazil to other former Portuguese colonies in Africa, and with tourists and Brazilian immigrants to Portugal and other areas of Europe and Africa. Brazilian religions have become 'among the most appealing and widespread religiocultural forms and … Brazilians have become crucial players in the creation of global religious networks' (Oosterbaan, van de Kamp and Bahia 2020, 1). In part, Brazil has become a prime exporter of religions because many Brazilians have migrated to other areas of the world in the last two decades (Oosterbaan, van de Kamp and Bahia 2020, 1). Brazil is also often imagined by Americans and Europeans as a '"cool territory," an authentic tropical, spiritual, and sensual place', and thus attracts tourists who export its distinctive spiritual traditions (Oosterbaan, van de Kamp and Bahia 2020, 3; Rocha 2017, 2020). Brazil's relative prosperity has, in addition, allowed it, like Nigeria and South Korea, to be a major mission-sending nation, and Brazil has at least two Pentecostal churches with extensive mission outreaches to Europe and Africa—the Universal Church of the Kingdom of God (UCKG) and the World Church of the Power of God (Freston 2005; van de Kamp 2016a). Because these Brazilian churches offered services in Portuguese, they spread first to former Portuguese colonies like Mozambique and Angola (Premawardhana 2018; van de Kamp 2016a). But Brazilian churches now also have a large presence in non–Portuguese speaking areas of Africa such as South Africa (Freston 2005; van Wyk 2014).

In some ways, the Word of Faith movement also exhibits the decentred Pentecostal pattern. The movement originated in Oklahoma and Texas and was associated with a group of closely affiliated pastors including Oral Roberts, Kenneth and Gloria Copeland, Kenneth Hagin and, more recently, T. D. Jakes and Joyce Meyer. But the movement has spread worldwide and some of its best-known proponents, such as Paul Yonggi Cho (South Korea), the late Myles Munro (Bahamas), Edir Macedo (Brazil) and Reinhard Bonnke (Africa), work from outside the US.

While religious globalisation now flows 'from everywhere to everywhere', it is a subject of debate whether decentred religious globalisation has produced significantly new visions. It has now become commonplace to note that the demographic weight of world Christianity has shifted to the global south and that southern hemisphere Christians can be expected to have a growing impact on Christian belief and practice. Anderson (2004, 2013) suggests that Pentecostalism, the fastest growing kind of Christianity, allows for Christianity to be shaped by local concerns and beliefs since Pentecostal churches often do not require extensive training for pastors. Consequently, Anderson predicts that the demographic shift in world Christianity will produce significantly new visions. Jenkins (2006) also argues that, as the demographic centre of Christianity shifts south, views of Christians from outside Western Europe and North America, where a common experience of poverty and marginalisation creates similar interpretations, will increasingly shape world Christianity. For instance, many African churches emphasise Old Testament accounts of famine and hardship that resonate with real experiences in people's lives, and many prefer socially conservative messages.

Sanneh (2003), similarly, suggests that Christians from the periphery will read Christianity in view of their own spiritual and social realities; since church leaders from Africa, Latin America and the Pacific do not come from a position of power and are racially and ethnically diverse they will not promote visions that support global, racial and economic hierarchies. Writing from the perspective of the Anglican Church, Nazir-Ali (2009, 33) argues that the gospels are always localised as people use them in the context of their own life circumstances, and that the early Christian church involved missionary outreach from churches in Asia and Africa. The translatability of gospels in light of local circumstances is crucial and no one culture should monopolise the interpretation of the Bible (Nazir-Ali 2009, 34).

But it is not clear that churches from the global south always or even usually contest Euro-American ideologies. The success of religions from the global south often depends on the extent to which they fit into pre-existing global 'assemblages' dominated by wealthier countries (Rocha 2013, 2020). For instance, the John of God healing movement in Brazil attracts many Europeans, North Americans and Australians because they see the movement as part of well-established new age networks and beliefs and, in fact, only embrace those aspects of the John of God movement that fit into the Euro-American, new age belief system (Rocha 2013, 2017, 2020). The John of God movement also appeals to affluent Euro-Americans because it fits with a 'Global North imaginary of the Global South as redolent of spirituality … [and as] the primitive, traditional, exotic other' (Rocha 2020, 217). In short, religious movements from the global south may succeed with Euro-Americans to the extent that they fit into their preconceptions and do not necessarily alter those preconceptions.

Further, missionaries from the global south often endorse Euro-American ideas about individual initiative and self-monitoring as the key to success instead of challenging structural sources of inequality. For instance, the UCKG, a Brazilian Pentecostal church with branches in Africa, focuses on freeing individuals from the influence of 'demonic spirits' linked to community and extended family ties and traditional practices. Once freed from demons and pressures from extended family, believers can become entrepreneurs and succeed financially (van de Kamp 2016a; see also O'Neill 2010 on Guatemalan Pentecostals; Kim 2015 on Korean Pentecostals). Kim (2015), similarly, found that South Korean missionaries in the United States accept American racial hierarchies and views of economic development and progress. South Korean missionaries pass over African Americans to focus their efforts on white Americans who they think are more influential. South

Koreans see Americans as having brought the blessings of development and modernisation to South Korea and hope to give back to Americans the spiritual commitment that they once had and have now lost. Likewise, O'Neill (2010) found that the El Shaddai megachurch in Guatemala, which was heavily influenced by Paul Yonggio Cho's South Korean church, promoted individual self-discipline and self-monitoring as key to national development and stability.

Churches from the global south also often endorse the same world hierarchies and stereotypes as Euro-American churches with whom they interact, since they participate in the same global religious assemblages. O'Neill (2010, 170–78) argues that the world community envisioned by Guatemalan Pentecostals and their counterparts in other nations is an 'international' rather than 'transnational' one in which national identities and stereotypes are prominent; Pentecostals speak of relationships between nations and often promote pride in essentialised national identities, as well as endorsing racial hierarchies within and between nations. For instance, urban ladinos in the Guatemalan El Shaddai Church endorse ethnic hierarchies when they set out to help rural Mayans—conceived as childlike primitives who need to be taught such things as good hygiene, time management and other habits so that they can develop rural businesses (O'Neill 2010, 159–66).

The UCKG is an interesting case study of the ways religious flows from 'south to south' do and do not differ from the traditional mission of 'the West to the rest'. The UCKG is one of the fastest growing churches in South Africa with churches in all major towns and cities and a membership of between 400,000 and 1 million; although, many people join the church for short periods, seeking solutions to specific problems, and then leave, so it is difficult to estimate total membership (van Wyk 2014, 235). The appeal of the UCKG to Africans has little to do with solidarity between Brazilian pastors and Africans or with contesting global racial hierarchies. UCKG pastors see Africa as the heart of all evil and believe evil spirits came to Brazil with African slaves and became part of the possession cults Candomble and Umbanda. To free the world of demonic possession, the UCKG sends pastors back to Africa to combat these powerful spirits (van de Kamp 2016a, 9). Freston (2005, 47) described Brazilian pastors as 'ethnocentric and lacking in empathy with … host populations'. Crivella, a Brazilian UCKG bishop, portrays Africans as 'very superstitious' and 'simple' people who are easily misled by traditional healers (Crivella 1999, 40–53, cited in van Wyk 2014, 16). The UCKG in South Africa pays local pastors less than Brazilian pastors (van Wyk 2014, 16). Higher-level positions in the church's transnational structure are all held by Brazilians while Africans were employed mostly as assistants and auxiliary pastors, again suggesting a lack of cross-cultural solidarity (van Wyk 2014, 67). The UCKG frequently moves its pastors so they seldom form strong bonds with members of the congregations in Africa (van de Kamp 2016a; van Wyk 2014, 62). Pastors are focused on 'the UCKG's larger spiritual project of trying to outmanoeuvre and defeat Satan' rather than on shepherding local congregations (van Wyk 2014, 67).

Nevertheless, Brazilian pastors' status as 'both insiders and outsiders to the spiritual world in Africa' makes the church very appealing because 'Brazilian missionaries' simultaneous knowledge of, and break with, the Afro-Brazilian spirits demonstrate[d] their experience with the real nature of "evil" spiritual beings and their power to overrule them' (van de Kamp 2016b, 246). One person told van de Kamp that, unlike Western missionaries, 'the Brazilians understand these things of *magia negra* (black magic)' (van de Kamp 2016a, 7). UCKG pastors draw on their knowledge of West African spiritual beliefs and practices and know little about local beliefs in other parts of Africa. But their lack of specific knowledge is viewed as making it safer for pastors to contest ancestral spirits without risking being attacked themselves (van de Kamp 2013, 254). Van Wyk found that South Africans also liked the emphasis on driving out demons because they also believed that misfortune was caused by evil spirits (van Wyk 2014, 139).

Because of their status as partial insiders who understand ancestral spirits, UCKG pastors are able to advocate individual choice and the nuclear family over extended family, offering themselves as examples of believers who have been able to journey away from their culture to adopt a new 'modern' way of life (van de Kamp and van Dijk 2010, 11; van de Kamp 2013, 356). In Mozambique, van de Kamp found that a growing population of well-educated successful urban women attributed marital misfortunes to rural relatives manipulating ancestral spirits. Women 40–50 years old came of age during a socialist era during which ancestral rituals were banned and so had little knowledge of these rituals. But people felt that ancestral spirits, and members of the extended families involved with the same spirits, had power over their lives. This drew them to Brazilian pastors who offered ways of combating spirits and models of people who had broken free from such demons (van de Kamp 2012, 438, 2016b, 18). Women who wanted to transform their lives and break free of local gender roles were drawn to Brazilian churches whose focus on overcoming African spirits 'offer[ed] possibilities for transcending the local' (van de Kamp 2016b, 28).

The UCKG case, in short, suggests that south–south religious flows may generate different kinds of connections than those between north and south. But the nature of these connections varies according to situation and the groups involved do not always feel commonality and they often embrace Euro-American ideas about modernity and progress. Consequently, the south–south mission does not necessarily promote a common identity as members of the global south or a common focus on world inequalities. Fijians and Tanzanians, for instance, told me that a common Fijian myth that Fijians had originated in Tanzania was clearly wrong since the two groups were so different. Further, local and national identities are generally reinforced when Christians from different areas of the global south interact.

Fijians and Their Transnational Networks

In the following pages, I argue against ambitious claims about Pentecostalism as a global force either for spreading or for contesting Euro-American modernity. Everywhere, Pentecostalism is incorporated into local projects so common language often masks significantly different practices. In the Harvest Ministry networks, ideas about community and individuality were shaped by the particular local circumstances in each place. Partly as a result, there was no particular connection or shared vision among Fijians, East Africans and Papua New Guineans as fellow citizens of the global south. Each group saw themselves as very different from the others and had, in fact, had substantially different experiences of colonialism and postcolonialism that prevented them from forming a sense of common opposition to former colonisers. Further, in each group, leaders were more interested in redefining their position in local society than in resolving world inequalities, a task that generally led them to emphasise local uniqueness rather than to stress a shared identity as global southerners. This process often involved drawing on the Euro-American imaginary of the characteristics of global southerners as childlike primitives with a natural capacity for faith and global northerners as rational but spiritually dead since this was a world semantic or 'assemblage' (Rocha 2020) that already had resources behind it.

3

The Harvest Ministry as an Exportable *Vanua*

One morning in 2012, as we were waiting for an early morning prayer breakfast to begin, my friend Luisa and I fell into conversation with Pastor Mosese, a former Harvest Ministry missionary who had been posted in Suva for the last three years and had recently learned that he was being transferred to Vanua Levu, Fiji's second largest island, to lead a church division there. I had talked with Pastor Mosese a few times before and I had always found him to be friendly and cheerful. This morning, however, Pastor Mosese seemed a bit low as he and Luisa chatted about the importance of submission in finding one's true calling and ultimate life satisfaction. 'I really thought my calling was to be a missionary', Pastor Mosese confessed:

> It was really hard for my wife and I when we were called home from overseas. We had to leave our congregation. We had started a Bible school there; we had to leave it.

So, he continued, he had come back home and taken charge of an important division (or ministry) at the Suva church. That had been very difficult because he had never thought that working in that area was his calling. But it had turned out that he liked the work and was very good at it. Now, however, he had been told by the senior pastor and the church council that he had been reassigned. The new post was an important one, but it would take him away from Suva where he and his wife had settled and where many Fijians prefer to live. 'It's really hard sometimes to submit', he said again:

> It's the hardest thing you will do to submit like that. But when you submit, then you understand your true calling and you find peace. It's really wonderful the peace that you feel when you have finally found your true calling.

He continued for my benefit, realising that I had little experience with being part of a church community:

> When you are born again, you will feel that peace. When you say that you are a sinner and you receive Jesus Christ as your personal Lord and saviour, you will have that feeling of peace. But really, that is just the first step. Then you go deeper, submit to the church, then that is really hard. You think you know what you should do but really you don't. It's really hard when people tell you to do something and you don't think that is right but you have to do it. But then when you submit like that and find your calling, then you really feel the peace.

Luisa politely agreed that sometimes people weren't able to perceive God's intentions and wanted to do things that were not in God's plan for them; this only led to frustration. God created each of us for a particular purpose and we would never be happy and prosperous until we stopped fighting Him.

I had been attending the Harvest Ministry in Suva and similar Pentecostal churches in other areas of the world off and on for about six years at that point and was familiar with the idea that each person had a calling, a specific purpose or role he or she was intended to play in God's master plan for His kingdom on earth. I had also often heard people say that unhappiness and misfortune resulted from failing to be where God 'wanted you to be', and, instead, pursuing things you mistakenly believed would make you happy. The idea that only an 'anointed man of God' further up in a church hierarchy would be able to perceive God's will was also a familiar one that I had heard from Fijian, American, Papua New Guinean and Australian pastors.

And yet I was still a bit taken aback at Pastor Mosese's words about submitting to authority this message was antithetical to the common stereotype of the flat Pentecostal Church where each individual had a personal relationship with Jesus (see Daswani 2015; Harrison 2005; Reinhardt 2014, 2015 on hierarchy and submission in Pentecostal churches).

In this chapter, I analyse the Harvest Ministry construction of leadership and community as a transformation of the model of the indigenous Fijian *vanua* laid in place during the British colonial period. Church leaders drew on the model of the *vanua* as it was defined through British indirect rule to imagine a hierarchical church community where pastors channelled vision and anointing to an obedient church community where everyone played his or her role. However, pastors portrayed the church as contesting the traditional Fijian *vanua* and justified their vision of leadership and community in terms drawn from transnational Pentecostalism and business. Pastors from Fiji, the US, Australia, New Zealand and other areas spoke of 'corporate anointing', in which a whole group, acting in unison, could experience a collective blessing that would make the church community greater than the sum of its parts. Often pastors linked corporate anointing to submission to a senior pastor who would maintain a consistent 'corporate structure' in the church that would allow him to effectively channel anointing to the congregation. The result was to redefine leadership roles in order to emphasise professional achievement and facility with the ways of transnational business and Pentecostalism. These new urban leaders were in charge of what, in many ways, looked like an urban, and potentially exportable, *vanua*, that is, a ranked community divorced from ties to land and locality.

In analysing constructions of community and self, I address a longstanding debate about the ways in which Christianity encourages rupture with pre-existing moral and social systems (Robbins 2007). Many Christians, particularly Pentecostals, stress the importance of rupture with past ways of thinking and living and hold 'discontinuity' models of history that emphasise radical disjuncture, such as when individuals choose to be reborn and create a new Christian self. Pentecostals also commonly encourage people to abandon past ways of life to adopt entirely new moral systems (Meyer 1999; Robbins 2004a, 2004b, 2007). While rupture with past ways is obviously important to Pentecostals, close examination shows that often such rupture is selective and can be 'resonant' such that new practices repeat some key aspects of old ways (Eves 2020; McDougall 2020; Macdonald 2020; Meyer 1999; Tomlinson 2010). Generally, people focus on leaving behind only certain aspects of the past while implicitly retaining many values, practices and beliefs. In Vanuatu, for instance, Eriksen (2008) found that the Presbyterian Church strengthened a 'silent', 'submerged' kind of sociality associated with women who forged ties between groups through moving, often when they married. At the same time, the church prompted rupture with male-dominated political forms rooted in patrilineal villages.

In the next two chapters I suggest that the Harvest Ministry emphasised rupture with certain aspects of past practice, such as hereditary rank, while retaining many other aspects of indigenous Fijians' ways, such as respect for senior males in a hierarchical community. I show that this selective and resonant rupture attracted successful urbanites through its focus on professional achievements and the qualities that people might need to succeed in professional life, such as the ability to fit into new contexts and present innovative ideas confidently. But the church's continued emphasis on the leadership of senior males was also attractive to successful male professionals. The selective rupture with past ways also appealed to many less successful people through suggesting that ordinary people could succeed through belonging to community, somewhat like the rural *vanua*, where a leader channelled prosperity to people who would not otherwise be able to achieve it.

Successful people contributed money to the church and received social recognition and spiritual blessings in return. They also internalised a way of looking at the world that taught them to see their lives as meaningful and blessed. The church used the money for numerous projects, such as building a primary and secondary school and to employ many less wealthy people including pastors and missionaries, at least some of whom were, as one pastor put it, 'simple village boys' who would not otherwise have had many jobs available to them. The church exchange system was also apparent on an international scale when, for instance, successful Papua New Guineans gave money to support young Papua New Guineans to go to Bible school in Fiji and to serve as missionaries in Africa. The benefactors often gave money to achieve spiritual blessings to protect themselves from what they believed to be curses directed at them by less successful relatives. The hierarchical church community, in short, worked well for many people partly because it drew on the well-established model of the *vanua*. But the Harvest Ministry reformulation of leadership and community also established a structure that was more hierarchical and authoritarian than the *vanua*. Eventually the church alienated a significant number of people for many of the same reasons that these people were disaffected from the *vanua*; that is, people thought that pastors were too authoritarian and that the church asked people to give too much money to its causes.

From *Mana* to Anointing

The Harvest Ministry construction of leadership and community both drew on and, in some ways, contested a model of the indigenous Fijian *vanua* laid in place during the British colonial era. Kaplan (1995), Tomlinson (2009), France (1969) and many others have shown how the emphasis on hierarchy and order in the indigenous Fijian *vanua* was jointly defined by high chiefs from coastal and island areas in the south and east of Fiji, and British colonial officials with overlapping interests in preserving order and supporting the privileged positions of Europeans and indigenous elites. Kaplan (1995) and Toren (1999) argue that the British and high chiefs from the coast replaced a model that emphasised reciprocal relationship between 'people of the land' who selected and installed foreigner chiefs 'from the sea' with a more hierarchical model, based on idealised images of the British aristocracy, which emphasised the power of benevolent and wise chiefs to bring prosperity and spiritual blessings to obedient subjects. When coastal chiefs such as Ratu Seru Cakobau converted to Christianity, they drew on an existing model of foreign chiefs from the sea bringing spiritual *mana* to subjects from the land to portray chiefs as channelling blessings from God to a submissive community; these constructions, however, were considerably more hierarchical than earlier ones. Colonial models also imposed a hierarchical model most typical in the south and east of Fiji on the whole country, even though societies in the western and interior areas of Viti Levu, Fiji's largest and most populated island, had been considerably more egalitarian (Kaplan 1995). High chiefs such as Cakobau praised the British for bringing transition from darkness to light and established an uneasy (Tomlinson 2009) alliance between Christianity, colonialism and indigenous Fijian elites from the south and east. These ideas validated the power of chiefly elites within Fiji and a racial hierarchy that placed indigenous Fijians, as partners in the 'civilising mission' of the British, above Indo-Fijians brought in as indentured labour for plantations (Kaplan 1995).

The British brought the invented *vanua* into law when they registered 83 per cent of Fiji's lands to clans where subordination to chiefs was assumed. Land that was registered to Fijian clans in the *Volai ni Kawa Bula* (Registry of Clans) could not be sold but could be leased to a growing population of freed Indo-Fijian indentured servants who grew sugar cane and other crops. Land rents were divided so that regional high chiefs (*tui*) and lineage leaders (*i liuliu ni mataqali*) received a disproportionate share of the land rents. The British also created a national Great Council of Chiefs with an important advisory role in government and selectively educated the children of chiefly families to take on positions in governments.

The British also later put in place village-level indigenous representatives of the colonial administration who enforced proper deference to chiefs and invented traditions. Village-level *buli* required villagers to contribute communal labour to maintaining roads, buildings and gardens for officials and chiefs, and could punish people who failed to follow these codes. The British established schools primarily for chiefly Fijians and left it to the Methodist Church to educate commoners in the rudimentary reading, maths and other subjects deemed necessary to farm and fish in villages. Villagers had to apply to the government for permission to migrate to urban areas.

These colonial-era restrictions resulted in a plural society and economy in which Indo-Fijians ran small farms and businesses while indigenous Fijians lived in villages and dominated the government bureaucracy, the army and the police force. Indo-Fijians' dominance in business was reinforced by a wave of Indians from Gujarat Province who came to Fiji as free migrants after World War II. The political system also reinforced ethnic pluralism. The British left in place a parliamentary system with 'racial' voting in which Indo-Fijians, indigenous Fijians and general voters (European or from other Pacific Islands) each had a designated number of parliamentary seats and voted for separate slates of candidates. Lawson (1996), Trnka (2008) and many others have argued that racial voting exacerbated ethnic tensions by creating a situation in which people feared that the other ethnic group would dominate government if the vote within their own ethnic community split. In this situation, people focused on common ethnic interests and were less aware of economic commonalities that cross-cut ethnic divisions. The racial voting system remained in place, with some modifications, until 2014 when Bainimarama eliminated it and declared all Fijian citizens equal regardless of ethnicity.

Throughout the colonial era and after Fiji became an independent country in 1970, the special spiritual and communal nature of indigenous Fijians, as embodied in the hierarchical *vanua*, became a key symbol justifying indigenous control of land and a privileged position in government over a large Indo-Fijian population. But it worked less well for a growing population of urban, non-chiefly, indigenous Fijians after laws requiring people to stay in villages were relaxed and education was extended through affirmative action policies. The ideology supporting chiefly leadership became less attractive after Bainimarama began to chip away at chiefly privilege by abolishing the Great Council of Chiefs and the system of allocated land rents that favoured chiefs. He also banned large assemblies of the Methodist Church, which generally supported *vanua* hierarchy, after some church leaders criticised his administration.

Participating in Pentecostal churches was one avenue for critical re-examination of indigenous Fijian society. Pentecostal churches reaffirmed the special nature of the indigenous community as deeply spiritual people whose moral values should shape national policy, but suggested new ways to realise key indigenous values such as commitment to community and service to others (see also Brison 2007b). Pentecostal discourse emphasised commitment to community over individual gain, but created new kinds of urban, international communities divorced from the traditional landed *vanua*, thus convincing Fijians that their special communal nature made them global citizens par excellence. As Miyazaki (2006) says of Fijian Seventh-day Adventists, Pentecostalism implied that Fijians' distinctive culture could move them forward in the world, in contrast to Methodism, which portrayed Fijians as having fallen away from an ideal past state.

Pentecostalism also paved the way for a renegotiation of leadership roles to validate achieved professional success by linking the qualities necessary to succeed in business and professional life with those necessary to lead a community. Pauwels (2020) and White (2015) note that many Fijians are suspicious of chiefs who pursue personal profit since chiefs are supposed to act on behalf of the community. High chiefs often have many opportunities to profit due to their access to government and business circles, and people see the secular power of high chiefs as potentially beneficial to their communities. At the same time, people suspect that high chiefs often use their secular power for their own benefit. Lower-level village chiefs may be so hemmed in by communal expectations that few people want to take on the role, instead preferring to pursue jobs in urban areas or build agribusiness; roles for which they often, in any case, earn more respect from relatives (Erasaari 2013).

More generally, many indigenous Fijians see business and professional success as antithetical to indigenous values. Those who save their money to reinvest in business or charge high prices for goods and services are considered *magimagi* (stingy). This quality is often associated with Indo-Fijians and Europeans whose ability to run businesses successfully is seen by many indigenous Fijians as reflecting lack of concern for community (Trnka 2008; Williksen-Bakker 2002). Williksen-Bakker (2002, 2004) interviewed indigenous Fijians running businesses ranging from a chain of bread shops to market stalls and found that many people felt that it was difficult to balance demands to contribute to community events (*oga*) and to give to relatives with the financial and time requirements of building up a business. Fijians often contrast the slow pace of work in villages where sociocentric values require people to be willing to put aside work for ceremony and conversation with the time regimentation required in professional and business life (Erasaari 2013, 2017). Williksen-Bakker (2004) found that some small-scale entrepreneurs hired others to run their market stalls because they were ashamed to be seen running a successful business. People also said that succeeding in business and professional life required confidence, a trait that was difficult for many indigenous Fijians to manifest since they were required to show shame/restraint (*madua*) as a mark of respect for elders.

Churches like the Harvest Ministry legitimise professional and business success by suggesting that innovation, time management and putting aside respect for elders and tradition are qualities that help to spread God's kingdom on earth. Professional success and the qualities necessary to achieve it, in short, are not selfish but are paramount communal values since they allow individuals to move beyond the *vanua* to play their role in God's world. While chiefs channel *mana* to a local community, Pentecostal pastors and successful professionals channel anointing, a powerful global force, to both the local church and the world at large. The move from *mana* to anointing, however, also produced a more hierarchical view of community in which those who had achieved success dispensed largesse to support less successful people who in turn performed spiritual labour.

The Harvest Ministry and the Methodist Church

The Harvest Ministry sermons contested the *vanua* through implicitly challenging Methodist conceptions about person and community. This was not surprising since the majority of indigenous Fijians were Methodists so church outreach understandably emphasised differences from Methodism. The Methodist Church was also closely intertwined with the vision of the *vanua* laid in place by the British. Many of the Harvest Ministry pastors had also started as lay preachers for the Methodist Church. Methodist services and *sevusevu*, speeches that accompany presentations of kava that mark all ceremonial occasions and lifecycle events in Fijian villages, presented a similar message about person and community and were often performed by the same senior men. In both, agency accrued primarily to communities rather than to individuals and only to communities in proper order, with everyone respecting and obeying those above them in the community hierarchy, and respecting community and tradition. Harvest Ministry sermons appeared to contest Methodist ideas about community by encouraging individuals to transcend traditional ways and community ties to find their calling in God's world. Closer examination, however, revealed that the Harvest Ministry community closely resembled the Methodist Church community and *vanua* in emphasising submission to leaders and the importance of belonging to a strong orderly community to ensure communal blessings of prosperity and health.

Methodist Church sermons emphasised the importance of an orderly community where everyone performed his or her designated role in a time-honoured communal structure. For instance, church services in Rakiraki generally started with a word of welcome (*vosa ni kidavaki*) to: 'You the senior men, you the senior women, you the young men, you the young women, you the children, sitting there today' (*Kemuni na turaga, Kemuni na marama, na cauravou, na gone yalewa kei na i solisoli, mai dabe tiko e daidai*). This formula directed attention to the key categories of the church and *vanua* where duties were assigned by age and gender. Senior men often served as lay preachers. Senior women led early morning prayers and sang the catechism before sermons. Junior men and women did less skilled tasks, such as cooking for visiting speakers, providing firewood to cook for feasts, cleaning the church and so on. Methodist services seldom addressed people with singular pronouns but instead used the second person plural for a large group, *kemuni*, addressing people as parts of larger groups such as the church community, the women of the church, then men of the church and so on (Brison 2007a).

Methodist sermons in Rakiraki also discouraged innovation, reminding people of the importance of preserving the traditional way of life laid in place by God and the ancestors. As Tomlinson (2009) found in Kadavu Province of Fiji, Methodist sermons often portrayed contemporary life as having fallen away from an ideal past order, leading to loss of agency. Church services often had a word from the *vanua* (*vosa ni vanua*) delivered by a senior male commenting on some community problem that generally involved failure to follow respectful practices. One Sunday, for instance, a senior man opened the Rakiraki church service by scolding the community for showing disrespect by shouting in the village instead of politely drawing near to people before speaking to them. On another occasion, a different elder spoke of how Fijians were now poor and powerless in their own land because no one wanted to farm as God had intended (Brison 2007a).

Sevusevu, similarly, implied that blessings of prosperity and health flowed to a community in proper order, with everyone performing his or her role in the ranked group. For example, *sevusevu* generally began and ended by tracing the chain of authority from lineage elders to local chief, to regional chiefs, to God and commended people for acting according to time-honoured custom by, for instance, 'loving each other and serving the lord' (Brison 2007a). After tracing the chain of authority, *sevusevu* frequently ended with a request for God to pour his blessings on the community now duly constituted in proper order. *Sevusevu* also emphasised that people were living on the land, and, indeed, house foundations, of their ancestors. Speakers often addressed remarks to the '*delai ni yavu tabu*' (literally tops of the sacred house foundations), that is, people who were living on their ancestral house foundations.

Methodist services and *sevusevu*, in short, emphasised that prosperity, health and agency flowed to communities of people living in the place of their ancestors, performing designated roles and following time-honoured traditions. Individuals were praised for subordinating personal desire to communal needs and customs and were criticised for acting in novel ways or trying to promote their own name and interests. People, for instance, spoke of the most beloved and respected community members as being humble, always sitting at the back in communal gatherings instead of taking their rightful place in the front; always being gentle and loving, never self-aggrandising; and being endlessly willing to contribute labour to communal causes such as preparing feasts, building community buildings and so on (Brison 2007a).

In contrast to the typical Methodist rhetoric, Harvest Ministry services, like those in many Pentecostal churches, emphasised making a radical break from the past, resisting social pressures and transcending local culture to find one's calling in God's kingdom. Individuals should strive for progress in their own lives and in spreading God's kingdom on earth, not for a return to an ideal ancestral state. Tomlinson (2010) says that Fijian political and religious leaders are often compared to Biblical prophets to suggest that their actions will return Fiji to the state intended by God. Harvest Ministry pastors, in contrast, liked to encourage people to be like Abraham and Moses, who had led their people into new lands and better ways of life. Pastors praised Abraham for making a clean break from Mesopotamia to become the father of God's chosen people. Likewise, they said that each individual believer had to leave behind his or her 'Mesopotamia', or past way of life, to find a new life with Jesus (Brison 2007b). Ultimately, however, the individual quest to transcend local culture was a communal one since the goal was to play one's particular role in creating God's kingdom on earth.

While the Methodist sermons frequently emphasised the ways that contemporary life had fallen away from a past ideal order, Harvest Ministry sermons advocated enterprise, initiative and progress that required learning not to be limited by one's upbringing. Harvest Ministry sermons painted a picture of individuals unable to think past accustomed ways of doing things to progress to new levels, feeling 'oppressed and depressed' because they lacked wealth and higher degrees. This construction implicitly critiqued the *vanua* as a place where people were limited by the need to express shame (*madua*) and respect (*veidokai*) in the presence of elders. In Harvest Ministry sermons, shame and respect undermined the individual confidence that was necessary to play one's role in God's world.

In a Sunday sermon in Suva, for example, Pastor Maka, one of the pastors assigned to the Suva church, told the congregation that most of the Harvest Ministry pastors had started out as 'simple village boys' without much education and had been able to progress through faith. They had followed God's will and had been able to transcend their circumstances. Pastor Maka said:

> Most of us when we started were just simple villagers … Many Christians today … we are so conscious of sins, guilt, failure. That's all we are conscious of. But we should be retrained from being sin-conscious, defeat-conscious, failure-conscious, into a new consciousness where we can realise that the creator of the universe is living in us … It takes you away from guilt, from shame, from defeat and you begin to live in a new consciousness, 'GOD is in me!' and grow in this realisation. You will begin to walk in a new stride, there is a spring on your feet … Reverend Vili started from nothing. He was unknown. He used to walk around with his shoes lined with *Fiji Times*. Not the way we know him. But he started to work by faith and God blessed him.

Pastor Maka's words also signalled the extent to which Harvest Ministry sermons were located in a wider world than the *vanua*. They evoked a listener who had started, like the Harvest Ministry pastors, as a 'simple', 'uneducated' person in the village and had the potential to leave the village, get educated and have an impact on the wider world if only he or she could escape the demoralising impact of the *vanua*. This was an inversion of the typical Methodist message that people were proud and selfish and needed to learn to sacrifice the self to take on their role in upholding village tradition (Brison 2007a).

Pastor Vili spoke on similar themes during a Sunday service when he implicitly critiqued traditional village culture and the Methodist Church, saying that Fijians were held back from being world leaders by 'poverty thinking' and too much gossip. This construction inverted stereotypical indigenous Fijian values by suggesting that serving the community, being willing to set aside time for social activities, and respecting leaders and tradition prevented people from achieving success in God's world community. While the Israelites were exiled in the desert after leaving Egypt, Pastor Vili commented, God had sent them 'fresh manna from Heaven' every day because they were living in a harsh environment. But when they had arrived in the promised land with its fertile soils, God had expected them to work, and so Fijians should realise they had plenty and shouldn't be lazy and sit around gossiping—a common criticism of people in villages—but should work. He told of how he had caught freshwater prawns as a boy to sell them to make a bit of extra money. He said Fijians were like the Israelites in the Promised Land; they already had been blessed with rich land so now they should work.

Pastor Maka similarly told the congregation one Sunday that they could all become world saviours. After talking about how Pastor Vili had started with nothing, lining his shoes with newspaper, Pastor Maka stated:

> And the world is becoming a better place for many people because of his ministry. He decided at the very beginning that he was going to take the word of God as his final authority. And because he did, the rest of us are here today … I want you to know that even if today it may be unknown to you, the hand of God is upon you. You are in a place of preparation today. I want to tell you that sitting here today are many world saviours, sitting here, I'm telling you, your moment will come. Your time will come.

Harvest Ministry discourse of the 'oppressed and depressed' person who needed to gain vision and faith to accomplish great things in a world community, in short, implicitly contested the Methodist discourse of wilful, selfish Fijians who experienced a loss of agency by failing to play their role in the *vanua*. Pastor Maka, like Pastor Vili, inverted stereotypical indigenous values by suggesting that respect for elders and tradition prevented people from playing their roles in God's world.

While Methodist sermons were spoken in Fijian, praised traditional customs and reminded people to play their role in the *vanua*, Harvest Ministry sermons prompted Fijians to think of themselves as part of a world community. Traits that Methodist sermons praised as upholding the *vanua* were ones, in Harvest Ministry sermons, that prevented people from achieving God's purpose for them in advancing his kingdom on earth. Sometimes Sunday sermons were 'themed' to particular countries and church members were instructed to come in costume from that nation. At the large annual Family Day fundraiser, each of the church zones represented a particular country of the world, attempting (not always successfully) to dress in the designated country's distinctive ethnic costumes and to perform ethnic dances. Pastor Vili spoke of the global Christian community in one sermon:

> I really believe the face of Christianity has dramatically changed over the years. Before we always say that there's a black church, a white church; there's an Indian church, a Fijian church … [Now] it's not a white church or a black church; it's a multicultural congregation (applause) … God is building up his congregation; He's building up His church and the Bible says the church of Jesus Christ it will be multicultural because the Bible says that in Heaven there will people from every language, from every nation, from every tribe and every town and we all will be singing together, amen! I just wonder what language we will be singing in Heaven? … I don't know if we will be singing in Fijian or if we will be singing in Hindi, but there will be a heavenly language that God will give to each one of us. We are in the same church and that's the beauty of what we are doing here at this very moment and you must understand that we are no longer a local church but we are a global church, amen! We are a global congregation and this will be a global movement. Every pastor is a global pastor; every leader is a global leader. Amen!

In another sermon, Pastor Vili again emphasised the importance of a transnational community, telling people that they needed to understand that their own culture was only 'valid within the context' of their 'boundary'. While Methodist discourse in many ways defined proper Christian behaviour as following traditional indigenous Fijian ways, Pastor Vili reminded people that the church had engaged in a great struggle to get away from the 'lowering' of the church to the 'level' of local society and instead to 'raise' it up to God's level through following the practices of a universal kingdom culture:

> There is only one culture that supersedes every culture and that is the kingdom culture ... We must liberate people from these cultural norms, which are not Biblical and so many times we accept them, you know, we talk about contextualisation. I really believe in contextualisation; but we must not contextualise the scripture to lower the scripture down to our level. We have to learn to rise up to God's level ... Just look back about 20 years ago, 15 years ago. Not only Fiji, in the Pacific, we were ridiculed; we were accused. We have fought this battle through and today the Holy Spirit is moving in our land ... We arrived at the place where we are, and the church in Fiji is in the place it is today, because we determined in our hearts in the very beginning that we have to enforce the kingdom cultures and the kingdom value into the hearts and the lives of our people.

Here Pastor Vili emphasised that the Harvest Ministry pastors had had to fight against Methodist village culture in order to 'rise up' to God's level to become part of God's kingdom culture.

Harvest Ministry rhetoric also located listeners in a transnational community by using metaphors drawn from management discourse, common in transnational Pentecostal language, again suggesting that the traits necessary to succeed in business, such as ability to manage time and money, were more Godly than traditional Fijian values. Pastor Vili, for example, talked about the importance of having a clear vision for one's life and sticking to it, realising that one's time was limited:

> We have to be enterprising and redeem our time so that all of our time is productive, amen? ... So many times we can get involved [and do not accomplish anything]. You need to have a clear vision and a clear purpose for your life. We need to match everything we do in life with a purpose, everything must contribute for added value ... We need to cut off all the things in our life that don't contribute to that purpose you know, so we can see our strength, our purpose. Do something that is useful.

Here Pastor Vili used management language such as 'added value', 'clear vision' and 'enterprise' to stress the importance of progressively improving one's own life and the world as a whole. Both Methodist and Harvest Ministry rhetoric praised those who worked hard and were useful to a larger community. But Harvest Ministry sermons suggested that values and attitudes believed to lead to success in business, such as time management and innovation, were more Godly than those associated with the *vanua*.

The Harvest Ministry as an Urban and Exportable *Vanua*

Harvest Ministry and Methodist sermons also had many common themes, suggesting that the transformation in ideas about person and community was more limited than first appeared. The Sunday morning English services that served partly to recruit new church members often emphasised individual empowerment. But sermons aimed at church members, such as the Tuesday night leadership training service for cell and zone leaders, frequently took a more authoritarian tone, stressing the importance of an orderly community and submission to leadership.

I heard several sermons in Suva about the importance of respecting leaders in July and August 2010 when there was conflict over Esiteri, a woman who had claimed to have received revelations from the Holy Spirit that the pastors were greedy and were asking for too much money. In these sermons, it was evident that innovative thinking and the ability to speak out confidently were traits that only senior males were expected to exhibit. Pastor Edward, one of the pastors assigned to the Suva church, warned his audience at the Tuesday night leadership training service not to pay too much attention to those who claimed to have received messages directly from the Holy Spirit. He said ordinary Christians did not have the maturity to distinguish messages that came from the Holy Spirit from those that came from the Devil. Those who criticised leaders, he continued, were motivated by the Devil and if one encountered such a person, one should report them to the senior pastors in the church and then keep one's distance from the gossiper. Pastor Edward warned his audience to watch out for 'Jezebels' among them, that is, people who were trying to destroy the church community by attacking leaders through claiming powers of prophecy. Speaking in tongues could be deceptive; one should not trust individuals who said they had received messages straight from the Holy Spirit, but instead should make sure that those so-called revelations were properly vetted by the church leadership. Pastor Edward said:

> Remember Jesus said Jezebel she calls herself a prophetess. Beware of such false spiritual authorities in the church ... They undermine the authority of the senior pastor. When you hear someone ... begin to question ... This is how they will say it, 'If I were Pastor [X], I would not have done that. I would have done it this way.' When you hear someone speak that way, that's the spirit of Jezebel. You are speaking to Jezebel. If someone ... talks like that, that's the spirit of Jezebel, undermining authority ... Spiritual authority in the church is in the senior pastors, the leadership.

Pastor Edward went on to suggest that God worked through communities in good order, with congregations submitting to leaders who followed set procedures. Pastor Edward warned that it took research, training and experience to recognise a true revelation from God, so people should listen to pastors, not to individuals who claimed to have personal revelations from the Holy Spirit:

> God is a God of order. Order brings life and freedom. God's life is ordered; His will is ordered and He gives orders through things in order ... If you are having one big service and people are prophesying like this and that, that's disorder. That's chaos. That's not God ... In order for you to reach God you must first submit to man ... You can't just start preaching. You have to be under someone else's leadership. You have to [be] under someone else who can guide you. Someone that rebukes you; someone that can reprove you. So when people start coming in talking about spirits, speaking in spirits, it's very hard to tell them you have to listen to authority ... God has an order in the church and it is researched and researched and researched. However it is attempted, it is vital that it is a place in order. It is a place in order and it should be respected whether we agree or not, the governmental structure within ... Order is important because it keeps all forms of deception out.

Pastor Vili also emphasised submission to leadership in one of his Sunday sermons during this time. One should not just listen to any prophecy since the Devil was on the attack in these last days before the return of Christ, but, instead, one should defer to the judgement of experienced and trained leaders who were anointed by God; individuals were lost without the support of a real human community:

Some people will come and say, 'I just believe in the Holy Spirit.' Don't listen to anyone who says that. People who say that are demons. That person is a rebel. He is a witch. They are silly people. They do not understand the principle of the church. See the word church is mentioned about 140 times, 150 times in the Bible. Ten per cent of the word church that is mentioned in the Bible is the invisible church, the universal church … The invisible church, the unseen church, the spiritual church. But 90 per cent of the church that is mentioned in the Bible is related to local community, real community, real congregation, eh? Real leadership. You know you have to honour those above you: parents and their children, masters and their servants, husbands and wives … because your attitude towards those who are in leadership in the church reflects your attitude towards Jesus, your attitude towards the head … If you don't submit to those who you can see how can you submit to the Holy Spirit?

On another occasion, Pastor Vili again stressed the importance of being part of a hierarchical community, making the church sound very much like the traditional *vanua* where spiritual efficacy flowed through elders and chiefs down to a community where everyone was playing his or her proper role:

The anointing always come from the top down … there is a special anointing with the Harvest Ministry. There is a special anointing but every member must learn to be connected, to be connected. When you are disconnected it's very hard to allow that anointing to flow through you … You know sometimes I just really look around and see people struggling and I say, 'Why are they struggling? They are not supposed to be struggling.' The reason is because they want to disconnect themselves from the life, the flow, of the church.

In short, in many ways, Harvest Ministry discourse was very similar to Methodist discourse in stressing the importance of submitting to authority, being part of a community and taking on one's ordained role, or calling, rather than following individual desire.

However, the Harvest Ministry community, unlike the *vanua*, was not linked to any particular place, but instead was described as a transnational business and religious organisation. At one annual convention in Suva, for instance, an American pastor stressed the importance of reproducing one's productivity. The American Pentecostal bishop explained that first one created a successful product—a local church where anointing flowed and empowered everyone. Anointing, this speaker and several others had stressed, was something given to individuals to empower them to lead a healthy and successful life and to fulfil their roles in God's master plan for spreading his kingdom on earth. But anointing also came in a corporate form, such as when a group acted as one. This could be enhanced under the direction of a powerful man of God and a strong institutional structure. After achieving a strong local product, one institutionalised this structure, giving it a distinctive brand name, ensuring that people behaved in a consistent fashion so the brand would be recognisable and reliable. This process could potentially get one's church on the Forbes Top Ten list of charitable organisations (a list that this speaker invented for rhetorical effect). The next step was to 'reproduce one's productivity' by exporting one's successful brand to other places (Brison 2012).

A few weeks later, the Suva service began with a short ceremony commissioning five of the Harvest Ministry pastors to visit Latin America to hold month-long sessions to train their Latin American counterparts in the Harvest Ministry method of sending missionaries to groups of unreached peoples. Among those to be commissioned was Pastor Jone, a Fijian visiting Suva from his post in Port Moresby, Papua New Guinea. Asked by the senior pastor to 'share his heart', Pastor Jone spoke in resonant tones, announcing that it was the fulfilment of a life's dream to be sent on a one-month mission to Latin America. He declared that his mindset had been transformed and he was ready to take 'this product made locally to a global market'. 'The vision is so clear. I stand on the foundation of a million-dollar anointing,' he continued, referring to a fundraiser the day before when the church had raised over 1 million FJD to build a new secondary school. He concluded that he was ready to 'reproduce the productivity of the Harvest Ministry' in Latin America by training the pastors there in the Harvest Ministry method.

Detaching the community of blessing from the traditional landed *vanua* was a significant reformulation of indigenous Fijian notions of religious agency and social structure. As in the *vanua*, senior indigenous Fijian men were generally in charge. But these men were generally successful urban professionals, not rural elders. The emphasis on being productive and making something of oneself also reinforced the position of successful urban professionals by drawing attention to their achievements, which was also accomplished through making such people cell and zone leaders and by pointing out people's achievements in sermons. Pastor Vili, for instance, frequently mentioned that Pastor Tomasi had been an executive with an Australian bank before retiring to become a pastor in the Harvest Ministry. Another Suva pastor also held a job as a finance officer at the University of the South Pacific, which was always noted when this pastor was introduced.

The Harvest Ministry gave these urban professionals a status equivalent but superior to that of rural elders by claiming that these successful urbanites performed service (*veiqaravi*) and dispensed compassion (*veilomani*) in a world Christian community conversant in transnational business. Within Fiji, younger men, junior pastors and women submitted to senior male pastors and elders. In the Harvest Ministry's overseas churches, many Fijian missionaries started out with the premise that people from so-called unreached people groups occupied subordinate roles under the guidance of benevolent Fijians, a vision that was also emphasised in conferences in Suva. Papua New Guineans and East Africans who worked with the Harvest Ministry viewed themselves as equal partners. But, as I show in Chapters 6, 7 and 8, Fijian missionaries clearly started out with a view of a transnational *vanua* led by Fijians, a construction that was particularly appealing to affluent donors in Fiji who became leaders in an imagined transnational community.

As will be further explored in the next chapter, the church community prompted subtle but significant shifts in the social hierarchy when the reciprocal and shifting hierarchy typical of the *vanua* was converted into a more permanent hierarchy in which successful professionals sponsored less affluent church workers and received social recognition as benefactors and church leaders in return. In the *vanua*, people's status shifted depending on who else was present. In some gatherings, an individual could take on the role of the highest-ranking person but might be lower-ranking when someone more senior was there (Brison 1999). In the church community, on the other hand, the hierarchy was less likely to shift from context to context. The church community also established an imagined international hierarchy through positioning Fijians as spiritual guides to unreached peoples in other countries.

Fundraising and Leadership

The ways that the Harvest Ministry both drew on the model of the *vanua* and reformulated it to highlight the achievements of professional people and to convert reciprocity into hierarchy was evident when comparing Harvest Ministry fundraising events to Methodist Church fundraising that I witnessed in Rakiraki.

I participated in Family Day, an annual Harvest Ministry fundraiser for designated projects, in 2012 and 2013, when the church was raising funds to build a secondary school. In October 1999, I participated in the annual *Adi Vakamisioneri* fundraiser to support the Methodist Church in Rakiraki.

The Harvest Ministry and Methodist events had similar structures, with the community divided into groups that competed to raise the most funds. Each group was represented by a 'princess' who wore a banner and crown like a beauty queen and was generally either a pre-teen girl or an older woman. The princess associated with the group that raised the most money was crowned queen.

The crowning of a queen drew attention to the achievement of the whole group in raising money, but each individual family was expected to contribute a set amount and was criticised if they failed to do so (see also Erasaari 2013). Conversely, in both Harvest Ministry and Methodist fundraising, everyone knew that some people gave a great deal more money than others (see also Erasaari 2013). In Rakiraki, large contributions usually came from successful urban relatives who contributed individually but also gave money to some of their poorer relatives so that these people could meet their family obligation to contribute (see also Erasaari 2013). In the Harvest Ministry events, successful people in the group gave more money.

The structure of the Methodist and Harvest Ministry events also diverged in significant ways that illustrated the way that the Harvest Ministry drew on, but significantly altered, the Methodist *vanua* model. First, in Rakiraki, people competed as *mataqali* (lineages) where *vanua* membership and age hierarchy were emphasised. *Mataqali* were multi-generational groups where senior people were in charge. In the Harvest Ministry event, in contrast, the competition was between church zones to which people were assigned and within which age-based hierarchy was less clear than in *mataqali*. Church zones often contained people from the same extended family. For instance, the core of the zone I joined was four adult sisters with their husbands and children. Some zones also comprised people from regions in Vanua Levu, Paster Vili's home island from which the church drew many members. But church zones also grouped together unrelated people who lived in the same part of the city or had some other point of similarity. The zone I joined, for example, contained people of mixed ethnicity, many of whom did not speak Fijian well. Pastor Tomasi's zone contained many people from Papua New Guinea since he had lived there, and other zones brought together people who worked together. Consequently, fellow members in the Harvest

Ministry zones were more likely to be contemporaries so the kin-based hierarchy was less clear. For instance, in the zone in which I participated, the sisters interacted as equals and their parents belonged to a different zone. The other zone members were, like the sisters, adults between the ages of 30 and 45.

Group leadership was also different in Methodist and Harvest Ministry fundraising. In Rakiraki Methodist Church, fundraising *mataqali* had *i liuliu* (leaders) who had inherited their position. The contributions of successful urban relatives were acknowledged but credit was officially given to the *mataqali* and by extension to the *i liuliu*. In the Harvest Ministry, church zones were generally led by pastors or by successful professional people. In fact, pastors often selectively recruited successful people and encouraged their involvement in the church by making them zone leaders. As in Rakiraki, people with more money usually contributed more money to the group's donation. But in the Harvest Ministry, unlike in the Methodist Church, the prominent role of wealthier donors was acknowledged since they were often zone leaders.

Finally, Rakiraki Methodist Church fundraising emphasised the *vanua* since people competed as members of village *mataqali*. The Harvest Ministry Family Day, on the other hand, emphasised the churches, participation in a larger world community since each zone was assigned to represent a country where the Harvest Ministry had missionaries and participants dressed in the colours of the flag of that country.

In short, fundraising constructed new communities and kinds of leadership for urban professionals in much the same way as sermons, drawing on the *vanua* model and transformed it in significant ways.

4

Reciprocity in the Harvest Ministry Community: Money and Spiritual Agency

'I just empty out my bank account. When you do that, it's awesome the way you will be blessed,' Sunil told me as we drove through Suva to attend a Family Day fundraiser. Sunil was one of the most active Indo-Fijian members of the Harvest Ministry. He told me that he had joined the church because he was attracted to its empowering, optimistic message and lively youth services. As we chatted on the way to Family Day, Sunil explained that the previous year the seven or so families in Sunil's church zone had donated almost 40,000 FJD, more than many larger zones. I asked him how they had managed to raise that much money. 'Well to be honest,' Sunil responded:

> It's mostly just me. I give about 80 per cent of the money for our zone. When you empty out your bank account it's amazing. You will be really blessed. You should have seen me when I started 15 years ago. I had nothing. Now look at me: I have four houses, three cars; the business is booming. When you sow your seed then you will connect to the anointing and be really blessed.

He paused, then continued:

> You know also, with all these people migrating out of Fiji since the coup there is not much competition. We small businesses are all doing really well because all the competitors are gone.

After a few minutes he went on:

> Last week when I was out of town with that church crusade they asked my wife to come sit at the head table at the church dinner for the guest speaker. She didn't like it; she said she didn't want to be that kind of big shot person. But for me, it's great.

In this chapter, I examine the appeal of the Harvest Ministry for successful professional Fijians like Sunil and to the many less successful people who contribute spiritual and other labour to the church. I then turn to the people who were initially attracted to the church but then left again. Many scholars have noted the appeal of the prosperity gospel to the poor who are drawn to the apparent promise of access to material wealth otherwise beyond their grasp (for example, Comaroff and Comaroff 2001). Fijians who did not belong to the Harvest Ministry also thought that people joined the church because they were duped into thinking they would get rich. My introduction to the Harvest Ministry, in fact, was through being told by friends in Rakiraki about the 'crazy' members of a particular Suva church who had sold all of their belongings in order to build the central church. I also heard a lot about the Harvest Ministry from members of the family with whom I stayed when in Suva. This family had a few relatives who belonged to the church, none of whom were very prosperous. They scoffed about one cousin who regularly attended the English services to show, according to my host family, that she was a 'big shot', even though she didn't understand English well enough to follow the sermon. They also said that she had given a lot of money to the church thinking she would get rich. The grandmother of the household, a staunch Methodist, was particularly disapproving saying that the Harvest Ministry 'brainwashed' people through music and dance and then convinced them that they would get rich if they gave money to the church. She said that one should give money to support church causes because this reflected good Christian values of caring for others, not because one expected some material return.

Prosperity churches also, however, appeal to affluent people because the belief that financial success is a sign of God's favour legitimises differences in wealth and offers people a justification for resisting requests for money from less successful relatives (Bowler 2013, 53; Brouwer, Gifford and Rose 1996; Gewertz and Errington 1999; Harrison 2005; Hunt 2000; van de Kamp 2016b). The attraction of prosperity churches to both wealthy and less wealthy people may also have less to do with money than with the support communities these churches provide (Harrison 2005; Premawardhana 2012; Wiegele 2004).

In Suva, the Harvest Ministry attracted many successful urban professionals, many of whom were related to Pastor Vili and his wife, Nau (mother) Sera or were fellow 'old boys'—that is, alumni of one of the elite boarding schools for chiefly indigenous Fijians established by the British. One pastor told me that Pastor Vili encouraged them to recruit government officials and bureaucrats and people who worked in banks and other important jobs. Pastor Tomasi, who had been a successful bank executive before retiring early to work with the church, told me that he had joined in part because the senior pastor had been very solicitous. This confirmed the idea that the church recruited successful people. On the other hand, there were also many less prosperous church members, some of whom received support from the church community and contributed to it in other ways, such as by giving spiritual guidance, working in the church and so on.

Observing devoted Harvest Ministry members over a number of years suggested that the main appeal was not economic prosperity but being valued members of a strong community. As Pastor Vili put it in one of his favourite sermons, which I heard a few times between 2010 and 2012, financial prosperity was only part of God's intention for obedient Christians. God also wanted people to prosper spiritually, relationally, physically and emotionally. The church helped to create this holistic prosperity through the exchange of money for spiritual guidance and social recognition, and through encouraging people to see themselves as blessed—supported by God because they were playing a meaningful part in His world. Wealthy people contributed money and received social recognition and spiritual and pragmatic support in return. For instance, Sunil spoke about prospering through emptying his bank account and donating to the church, but then talked about pragmatic reasons (such as hard work and the out migration of competition) for his success and went right on to speak of the social recognition he had received in the church. As I explore in the next chapter, Sunil and others also internalised narratives that empowered them by helping them to see themselves as blessed and as powerful contributors to a world community. Talking to committed members of the Harvest Ministry over the years suggested that the church community created an environment where people whose lives were largely urban and cosmopolitan could feel comfortable since at least some of the strict protocols governing behaviour in the *vanua* were relaxed. The church also allowed for subtle but significant shifts in gender and other roles. Finally, the church community brought together successful urbanites who could in some ways benefit from their connections with each other.

The money that wealthier people contributed supported, in turn, many less prosperous people who contributed to the church in other ways. Some of these people worked for the church as pastors, missionaries and other kinds of church workers. These people received financial support and contributed spiritual guidance. However, the church worked best for indigenous Fijians, particularly those who came from Pastor Vili's home island, Vanua Levu, or who were closely related to Pastor Vili or were alumni or the same elite boarding school he had attended. There were a few people like Sunil who were not indigenous Fijians who were centrally involved in the church. But, generally, people from other ethnic and regional groups tended to join the church for a few years and then leave again.

Successful Urban Professionals: Exchanging Money for Status

Sunil and his wife Vinaisi, an indigenous Fijian woman, illustrated the way the Harvest Ministry community functioned so that wealthier people contributed money and received social recognition, spiritual blessings and pragmatic support in return. Sunil and Vinaisi each assured me on several occasions that if one gave to the church 'sacrificially'—that is, beyond one's means—one would be awarded with abundant wealth. Vinaisi volunteered and she and her family had sold all their household possessions to donate money to build the Suva church. 'It really works,' she told me. 'You give it away and it all comes back.' Sunil told me several times that he always gave to the church even when he had no money in his bank account. Sunil was also generous with church members and friends, paying for expensive international flights for fellow church members and sponsoring a rugby team from his wife's village to go to Australia. He housed, employed and fed many young men from Vinaisi's village and hosted a family of Fijian missionaries for several months when they returned to Fiji for their furlough. Sunil assured me that it had paid off. Even though he said that he was less educated than his siblings, all of whom were still Hindus, he said he was doing better financially. His business was booming; he owned several houses and cars, and he always travelled first class.

In return for their generosity, Sunil and Vinaisi received social recognition. Sunil and Vinaisi seemed less interested in material items than they were in the standing they gained in the church community, which was much greater than they would normally have had in Fijian society since they were still in their early 30s and Sunil was an Indo-Fijian. When my student research assistants interviewed him, Sunil emphasised that he was a simple man living a simple life. Objectively, Sunil's house was comfortable but much more modest than houses of other people I knew with comparable incomes. On the other hand, he enjoyed a prominent place in church functions.

Sunil and Vinaisi also said that they received spiritual guidance and blessings from the church. Sunil alluded a few times to health issues that had plagued his family that he had left behind on conversion to the Harvest Ministry. He also had a close relationship with Pastor Edward, who had brought him into the church, and who was now a close friend and spiritual mentor. Sunil and Vinaisi often gave food and other forms of assistance to Pastor Edward to help support his large family. In the next chapter, I will show that Sunil also experienced himself as being blessed.

There were also pragmatic benefits to belonging to the Harvest Ministry, although neither Sunil nor Vinaisi talked about the church that way. At an early stage in my research, for example, Sunil suggested to me that giving money to the church was a good way to make connections, indicating that he understood the pragmatic impact of his donations. Sunil's business had flourished when he received a contract for a chain of banks; many local leaders in this bank belonged to the Harvest Ministry. Sunil also took a trip overseas with another church member who introduced him to people involved in manufacturing solar panels, in which Sunil wanted to invest. Sunil may also have benefited from employing young church members in his business. He told me once that small contractors like himself faced a constant turnover in employees. As soon as you trained someone to work in the business, he said, they would go off and sell their skills to someone else for higher wages. Through employing Vinaisi's relatives and fellow church members, he attempted to build a bond with employees to prevent them from leaving after he had trained them.

It was typical for prosperous church members to give both money and time to the church and to receive recognition and blessings in return. The leaders of my cell group, Luisa and Ropate, purchased a home with two flats through their church connections and, in turn, used one of flats to accommodate a widow and some young men from the church who couldn't afford their own housing. Ropate and Luisa also housed and fed a pastor from a remote island along with his wife and two children when they were in Suva for four months, and also took in short-term guests attending church events. In return, Nau Sera, the widow who lived in the upstairs flat, helped Luisa and Ropate to run their cell group and guided their spiritual development. Similarly, the pastor visiting from another island held regular prayer sessions for Luisa and Ropate and their friends. The church also paid for Luisa to do an early childhood education course after she spent many years volunteering in their primary school.

Ropate and Luisa also liked the way the Harvest Ministry helped to remove them, just a little, from their kin and peer networks. They still spent a lot of time with extended family but were able to avoid some of the more exuberant nightlife that went along with such relationships. The Harvest Ministry community established strict rules about personal behaviour that helped them to resist invitations to drink and stay out late (see also Burdick 1993; Chesnut 1996). Luisa and Ropate told me two different stories about their conversion from Catholicism to the Harvest Ministry that both stressed the ways that the Harvest Ministry had helped them to get away from a life of partying. Luisa told me that they had decided to join the Harvest Ministry after their daughter was born. She and Ropate had frequented nightclubs, leaving their infant daughter with her mother. One night, when they came back from the clubs, Luisa's mother had refused to let them take the baby, saying they were drunk and in no condition to look after her. Luisa said that they had been deeply ashamed and had decided to change their ways by joining the Harvest Ministry since Pentecostal churches, unlike the Catholic Church in which she had been raised, did not allow people to drink. On another occasion, she told me that they had decided to convert to the Harvest Ministry after Ropate had visited his sister in New Zealand and had seen how well she was doing. He decided, Luisa said, that he didn't want to waste his life, but wanted to accomplish something and so they could be surrounded by successful people who would help them get their lives in order.

Other people also mentioned that the church helped them to resist pressures to drink and to socialise, and helped to renegotiate gender roles. Mrs Vani, a primary school teacher and long-term member of the church, led a cell group with her husband. Mrs Vani told me that the Harvest Ministry had rescued her marriage by pulling her husband away from drinking with his friends (see also Burdick 1993). She told me that her husband had converted to the Harvest Ministry after going to jail; he saw Harvest Ministry pastors visiting other prisoners and admired the way they helped one of his friends pull his life together. Mrs Vani, herself, received recognition in the church as a cell group leader. When I asked to attend one of their cell group meetings, Mrs Vani told me that her husband had asked her to do the service because he thought that she was more articulate than him and so would do a better job. Mrs Vani also said that before she joined the church she had no purpose to her life; she just stayed at home with her children in the evenings. Now she felt that God was like a best friend, always with her, listening to her problems and meeting her needs. All she had to do was to think about something she wanted, like, for instance, a pair of yellow shoes, and that thing would appear in her life through some unexpected gift. Interestingly, Mrs Vani cast her pre-conversion life in a rather un-Fijian way, portraying herself as a lonely housewife, a description that didn't bear much resemblance to Mrs Vani's life, which included a household full of extended family members from outer islands who stayed for long periods of time. Mrs Vani's version of her life story suggests that Pentecostalism imports whole new scenarios and schema for understanding the self that help individuals to think of themselves as blessed, as I will outline in the next chapter.

The church also provided a supportive community for professional people whose life trajectories had taken them away from traditional Fijian village life. The church offered a community that included people with similar life experiences, and freedom from the many rules that structure behaviour in the *vanua*. Pastor Tomasi, for instance, told me that for most of his career as a bank executive in Fiji he had been a lay preacher with the Methodist Church. He had felt called to preach from a young age, partly because his grandfather had been an important Methodist pastor. He started attending the Harvest Ministry after Pastor Vili, an old friend from secondary school, had asked him to donate money to buy some chairs for the main church in Suva. He and his family attended the Harvest Ministry mostly as a courtesy, but he began to notice that his young daughters were much more enthusiastic when they attended the Harvest Ministry than they were at Methodist services. He was also impressed when his uncle became sick and Pastor Vili arranged to pray over the sick man immediately, in contrast to the uncle's Methodist pastor who said he couldn't visit the man for several weeks.

When Pastor Tomasi was transferred by his bank to Port Moresby in Papua New Guinea, Pastor Vili asked him to establish a Harvest Ministry church there, which Pastor Tomasi found he was able to do with great success. Later, when the bank wanted to transfer Pastor Tomasi to Australia, he decided instead to take a much less lucrative job with the Harvest Ministry in Suva. He had plenty of money, he told me, but wanted to spend the last years of his career doing something that he found meaningful. Pastor Tomasi and his family seemed to have found in the Harvest Ministry a community that they regarded as more congenial than the traditional Methodist *vanua*, perhaps because their lives had taken them so far from rural Fiji. The Harvest Ministry, which brought together business connections, old school friends and people within the banking community spanning several nations, reflected Pastor Tomasi and his family's social experiences and gave them a community of like-minded people. Pastor Tomasi and his wife led a weekly cell group meeting that was attended for the most part by Papua New Guineans living in Suva, again suggesting that the Harvest Ministry resonated with his transnational life experiences.

Similarly, Meri and Tukana, a Fijian couple running a small business in Papua New Guinea, found in the Harvest Ministry a community that spanned Papua New Guinea and Fiji and accommodated people like themselves who were not used to life in a rural *vanua*. Meri attended her first Harvest Ministry crusade in Papua New Guinea only because she was a secondary school friend of Pastor Vili's wife. She and Tukana were not yet married but were living together, supporting themselves with a compensation settlement Tukana had received after being injured on the job. They had moved to Port Moresby but found the economy there in bad shape and their resources quickly dwindling. Even though Meri was not very religious, she had been moved both by the Harvest Ministry crusade and by the fact the Pastor Vili had accepted her despite her unconventional lifestyle. Eventually, the couple worked through the church community to build their business through taking in young Papua New Guineans and training them in good business practices through supplying them with units of phone credit that they could sell at a slightly higher price. When I met Meri and Tukana, they were running several businesses and had been hired by several local companies to run motivational workshops on 'mindset transformation' for their employees, a method they had passed along to Pastor Inoke, a Fijian missionary in Kenya, to whose mission they gave money. I later encountered the couple in Suva where they were visiting Pastor Tomasi, an old friend from Port Moresby. In this case, the couple was integrated into a community of Fijians and successful Papua New Guineans in Port Moresby through joining the church, a community that also extended to Suva. The Harvest Ministry community gave them a group of friends similarly divorced from the social conventions of rural Fiji and Papua New Guinea and also networks that were useful for their businesses.

In Port Moresby, the Harvest Ministry appealed to a very small group of salaried professionals (many of whom worked with Fijians) who were, like Meri and Tukana, living lifestyles remote from those of their relatives in rural villages. One couple spoke to me at length about how they had joined the Harvest Ministry after their oldest daughter had developed severe epilepsy that had caused her to have to withdraw from school and to become severely depressed. They had visited doctor after doctor and had even taken her to Australia for treatment without success but had experienced some improvement in her condition by 'sowing their seed' to the church, first to an Australian church that they had seen on the Trinity Broadcasting Network and then to the Harvest Ministry. The couple hinted that they thought part of the problem was curses from rural relatives and they had tried to cut off all contact between their daughter and their rural kin. In Port Moresby, where they lived, a substitute community was provided by a small nucleus of Harvest Ministry elders. Their daughter had been invited by the Papua New Guinean senior pastor of the Harvest Ministry to his home base in Bougainville and was now employed in Meri and Tukana's flower shop.

Less Affluent Church Members: Exchanging Spiritual Work for Financial Support

The Harvest Ministry community also included many people who were not well off but were valued community members who contributed to the church through offering spiritual guidance and other kinds of assistance. The church, for instance, supported the family of one of its pastors who had died. His widow, Leba, rented a house at a low rate from another church member. The church also paid Leba's children's school fees and sponsored her eldest daughter to go on a one-year mission trip to China. Leba, in turn, worked in the Children's Ministry and housed a visiting Papua New Guinean woman who was attending the Harvest Ministry Bible College.

Pastors and missionaries also received support from wealthy church members and in return gave these people spiritual guidance. Missionaries returned to Suva for a six-month furlough every four years and stayed in the houses of affluent church members. Missionaries posted overseas often had contacts with local Fijians working for the UN and in other capacities, many of whom helped the missionaries in various ways. In East Africa, I accompanied a Fijian missionary and his family to Arusha, Tanzania, where they regularly stayed with a Filipino man working for the UN who was a co-worker of a Fijian who was also working for the UN. The Fijian missionaries held prayer meetings to help the Filipino man and his family with their problems while they were there. The family said that their involvement with Fijian missionaries helped both with spiritual guidance and with blessings to combat evil forces.

The church also provided careers for many people whose prospects would not otherwise have been great. Many pastors and missionaries were, as Pastor Maka, suggested, 'simple village boys'. Pastor Josua, a Fijian missionary in Tanzania, for instance, told me that he had met Pastor Vili, who was then a regional coordinator for Every Home for Christ, when he was a teenager in a village in Vanua Levu, Pastor Vili's home island. Pastor Vili had been impressed by Josua's speaking skills and employed him as an Every Home for Christ worker and sent him to Bougainville, Papua New Guinea. When Josua returned to Fiji, he applied to go to Tanzania as the Harvest Ministry's first missionary and won that post. Similarly, the Harvest Ministry recruited promising young people everywhere they had missions and found wealthy church members to sponsor these young people while they attended Bible college in Fiji. Several young Papua New Guinean men said that if you worked with the church, wealthy businessmen would pay for you to travel to Fiji and to other areas of the world.

In short, the Harvest Ministry was a close-knit community in which wealthy members contributed money that supported both church projects, such as building a primary and secondary school and sending missionaries abroad, and numerous less affluent people who worked in the church and provided spiritual guidance and blessings. Observing the Harvest Ministry over a number of years suggested that many of the core members of the church were related to the senior pastor and his wife, came from the same regions of the country as them or had met them at school. Many of the missionaries were from the home island of the senior pastor and had been given a chance at upward mobility through being incorporated in his church network. These core members felt a strong sense of loyalty to a cause they had been part of for many years that was an integral part of their careers and social networks. Many others, though, outside this core network, came to the church for shorter periods of time and then drifted away to attend less demanding churches.

The Costs of Submission

The Harvest Ministry eventually alienated a significant number of people. The frequent requests for money were almost as controversial among members of the congregation as among those who didn't belong to the church. I knew several people who had left the church because of pressures to give money. Often complaints about the requests for money were accompanied by complaints about the authoritarian leadership structure. I joined a cell group and church zone in 2010 and by 2014 the membership of the zone had almost completely changed twice, giving a rough sense of the tendency of people to join for a short time and then leave. The group had members from Rotuma, a Fijian island with a distinctive language and culture, several Asian Fijians and some people of mixed indigenous Fijian and other heritages. The high turnover of this group was perhaps an indication of the relatively weak outreach of the church beyond the indigenous Fijian community. Rotumans, some East Asian Fijians and people of mixed ethnicity, none of whom spoke Fijian well, were attracted to the church because, unlike many other churches, it offered English services. While the church welcomed such people, they were not generally integrated into the central core of the church unless, like Sunil, they were married to someone from that core group.

One couple, Cathy and Mark, who had attended the church for several years because they liked the music and the well-staged sermons, had largely stopped attending the church by 2014, although they continued attending cell group meetings until Cathy's cousin, Luisa, who led the group, tragically died. Mark was Chinese-Fijian. Cathy was of mixed ethnicity. Cathy joined the Harvest Ministry because she liked the way that the church stressed individual empowerment and spiritual experience. Mark followed Cathy, saying that he liked the lively and welcoming atmosphere in the Harvest Ministry.

The couple began to sour on the church after Cathy's friend Esiteri was expelled from the church because she claimed to have received revelations from God criticising the pastors. They both also disliked being pressured to buy 1,000 FJD shares in the Global Development Corporation. Mark told my research assistant in 2014 that he felt the requests for money were excessive and that pastors were sometimes just out to benefit themselves.

His words implied that the pastors were overly authoritarian, claiming to know what God wanted people to do, something that should be between each person and God:

> Every church has something good and something bad. [The Harvest Ministry] is very open [welcoming] to everyone, a very great church, but sometimes I don't like the fundraising, like money-wise. I [really] object to what they are trying to make it more for the funds for the church, trying to extend their own money through the church, this is totally wrong. Everything depends on what God is giving us to do. This is not church's job. I totally disagree with that. That is the only part I don't like. All our tithes and offerings, from the bottom of our heart, we [should] give it to our God, not forced by pastors or whoever. But it is wrong to say that you will get more blessings if you give more money. That is totally wrong. God know about us, what we want. I can't give my whole income to the church to donate. Even our God doesn't like it. He doesn't allow that.

Cathy told me that all the requests for money hindered her personal communion with God. She also found that members of the church could be hurtful and nasty to each other, a complaint that, again, suggested that church leaders were too authoritarian and that the church was not as welcoming to those who were not indigenous Fijian:

> I don't want to judge anyone but the very people you look up to, the mighty men and women of God, they tend to hurt people with their words, and that to me, I call that hypocrites. People are coming to be healed; people carry a wound with them. You know what they go through throughout the week. When people come to Harvest Ministry and experience that [hurtful talk], it is not a good feeling. And that is why some people today have stopped going to Harvest Ministry ... Well right now, given what happened on Sunday [when there was a long presentation about the Global Development Corporation], I don't even know about this Global Development Fund. I don't even know about the Global Development thing. I would just say it's gone worse. I think there should be some changes in there. Just come to worship God. Just come as you are. Stop demanding people to give. Let people have the free choice to give; let them have their free choice; don't try to demand. I have never seen a church that is so focused on money. Not about money; church is not about money. It is about saving a life, and it is all about God; it is all about Him. If He wanted a church to fundraise or something He would just, just bless someone with a billion dollars, and he would give the money to church because God spoke to him.

> It is wrong to demand every individual and child for money. That is a wrong thing I am looking at. It's wrong. I love the people, you know, but I am against what they are doing to the people when we come, we are in need of just the power of God.

Cathy had also been chagrined a couple of years previously when she and Mark were taken to a section reserved for overseas guests by the ushers one night when they attended the annual convention. 'I am not a guest; this is my church; I have gone here for five years,' she told the ushers. The church, Cathy complained to me on another occasion, clearly had some favoured core members and others like herself felt marginalised. Eventually, the couple withdrew from the church and Cathy decided instead to worship in weekly prayer meetings organised by Esiteri.

Through Cathy, I also met Esiteri, who was the 'Jezebel' targeted by the sermons in 2010, who, not surprisingly, was also disillusioned with the Harvest Ministry. Esiteri said that she had been a very active member of the church but had become disaffected over the years with the frequent requests for money. She described how the Harvest Ministry started raising funds in 'the millions', and encouraged church members to believe that by contributing they would see improvement in their life. In many years of contributing, Esiteri felt no closer to God and felt no improvement in her life. She said: 'I had never learned to hear the message of God.' She also felt in her heart that in order to improve her life she had to 'step aside from teaching and step away from being a worship leader in church'. She then became very ill and, after 10 months of going to doctors without getting better, had a near death experience where she experienced the presence of the Holy Spirit. When she began to share with others the joys of a personal relationship with the Holy Spirit, she was expelled from the church and church members were told to stay away from her. She concluded that the Harvest Ministry pastors had originally acted out of a covenant with God but had now gone astray. One did not need to submit to a church to find God but could speak to Him directly:

> [The Harvest Ministry] lost it. [At first God] had a covenant with the leaders of the Harvest Ministry and now they have gone the other way, their own way and don't follow the spirit of God. They do what pops up in their own mind ... God will send the great men of God with the message of the kingdom of God. Because you have the spirit of God in you, He will talk to you in a personal level. You will talk to Him, and say, 'Okay, I have been reading this in your word. The kingdom. But I don't know what it means.' He will teach

you, without even going to church. [The Harvest Ministry pastors] just decided to put that away and go on with their own program … They are doing their own fundraising for mission work. He is their provision. Why do you have to go and search for money and tire people and put burdens on the backs of people? And you keep using the word of God. No, our blessing comes from the hill of Cavalry [not from pastors who extract money].

As I travelled in Papua New Guinea in 2012, I also heard a great deal of grumbling from Papua New Guinean pastors about how the head church in Suva expected them to raise unrealistic amounts of money from their congregations and how some of the Fijian pastors placed too much importance on material possessions, always wanting to live in fancy houses remote from their congregations wherever they went.

The Harvest Ministry community, in short, worked best for those who sought a strong urban *vanua* to supplement or replace traditional networks that no longer reflected the reality of their lives. The church worked very well for prosperous and successful senior males closely allied with the senior pastor and for their families, who were treated solicitously and with respect. The church also worked well for less prosperous people, generally also from the core group, who were employed and otherwise supported by the group. But the church community was sometimes a less pleasant experience for young women like Cathy and Esiteri and members of other ethnic groups, indicating that, in many ways, the Harvest Ministry was less transformative than it claimed. The church embraced successful indigenous Fijian senior males but did not include younger women and people from other ethnic groups to the same extent.

5

Becoming Blessed: Learning a Charismatic Globalising Habitus

One rainy evening in Suva in September 2013, I sat in Ropate and Luisa's living room with 10 members of their Wednesday evening cell group. The room was nicely furnished with two couches and several chairs, but we all sat on the floor since there weren't enough chairs to go round and Fijians consider it rude to be physically higher than others. This evening we were joined by Sunil, Vinaisi and several young people who lived with them and worked in their business. After the opening prayers and hymns led by Luisa, we were asked to 'share' our 'testimony' about the movement of God in our lives over the last week. As usual, this request led to an awkward silence until Luisa, also as usual, started us off. She testified that she had had a massive headache in the afternoon and had thought that she would have to cancel the cell group meeting, but God had given her the strength and now she felt better. Luisa then proceeded around the circle asking each person if they had anything to share, which led only to giggles and downcast eyes and a valiant (but failed) attempt at testimony by a polite anthropologist, until Luisa reached Sunil. Sunil had just returned from a trip to Labasa, the largest city on Vanua Levu, and he spoke at length about his trip. He had been 'so honoured' to have been asked by Pastor Vili to go to Labasa to help with a crusade the church was holding there. He had arrived to find that the local organisers knew little about open-air rallies and had failed to set up the stage and the sound system properly. But Sunil had felt 'really blessed' because he was a contractor and was on hand to help them. He had spent the entire day helping to set up the stage and sound system for the crusade and then had been 'very blessed' when Pastor Vili invited him to eat dinner with him. The next day he and a friend had set out to visit a church on another part of the island but after about an hour he had received a phone call from Labasa announcing that the power was out there. 'We were so blessed,' Sunil continued, talking about how he got the call just before he had lost cell phone contact so had been able to turn around and drive back to Labasa to help out. In Labasa, he had to work quickly to find portable generators and was again 'richly blessed' when he happened upon a storeowner who had known his father and recognised Sunil from his boyhood and let Sunil borrow several portable generators without payment. The final blessing of the evening had been an invitation to sit on stage with Pastor Vili, although Sunil had been too busy running around making sure the generators were properly connected to make use of that blessing. So you see, he concluded, if you gave to the church you would be really blessed. People shouldn't worry about their lives; if they did what God wanted them to do, everything would work out and they would be blessed.

Scholars of prosperity churches note that many people are attracted to their optimistic, empowering message and may not expect material returns for their faith. Coleman (2000), for instance, points to images of Christ as a bodybuilder in the Word of Life Church in Sweden, saying that the main thrust of church rhetoric was not to promise material wealth but to encourage church members to see themselves as powerful actors in a transnational Christian community (see also Harrison 2005; Haynes 2017; Piot 2010). Luhrmann (2012), likewise, noted that Vineyard members often seemed to set themselves up for failure by praying for very specific things like job offers. But they were not discouraged when these things did not materialise. Instead, they were attracted to the Vineyard's systematic belief system prompting them to see the presence of a just and loving God in their lives.

In this chapter, I argue that Harvest Ministry members were encouraged to see themselves as blessed both when they succeeded and during difficult times. A series of devices helped individuals to see their lives as paralleling those of Biblical figures like Abraham and Job who, against all reason, maintained perfect faith that God would provide. Individuals who adopted such narrative strategies saw the hand of a loving God in their lives and, like Sunil, learned to see things like being called upon to rescue a badly organised crusade as blessings. They became happier and less anxious and were able to cope with adverse and novel situations such as multicultural work environments. Since happiness and peace were also seen as the mark of true faith, however, people learned to profess happiness and inner peace to display their strong belief whether or not they felt these emotions (Wilkins 2008).

Sermons linking adversity and blessing were particularly common in the sermons of missionaries and people working in overseas congregations of Fijians, such as those working for the British Army, because Fijians in other countries had to adapt to living in unfamiliar environments without the support of relatives, and often faced prejudice. But successful urban professionals in Suva like Sunil also faced new challenges and work situations, so sermons in Suva also frequently used devices to help people see themselves as blessed. The same discourse allowed a multinational community of professionals working for the United Nations in Arusha, Tanzania, and as managers in corporate farms to cope with the difficulties involved in holding transient jobs, working in unfamiliar environments with unfamiliar people without the support of networks from home.

As I will show in a later chapter, Papua New Guineans in the Harvest Ministry were drawn to the idea that they were 'connecting themselves' to a larger vision in which they could play a special role, as humble people used to physical hardship, in fulfilling the Great Commission. Experiencing themselves as especially valuable and blessed was more important than expectations of material prosperity.

Learning to Be Blessed

Luhrmann (2012) found that members of American Vineyard churches are taught techniques such as having conversations with God and learning to recognise some of their own thoughts as communications from God that help them to experience God's presence in their lives. As was evident in Pastor Mosese's story in Chapter 3, Fijians in the Harvest Ministry learned a way of viewing their lives that prompted them to see themselves as created by God to serve a specific purpose, or calling, in building His kingdom on earth. Like Pastor Mosese, each person learned that he/she had the characteristics necessary to fulfil his or her specific calling, but sometimes failed to understand 'where he/she was supposed to be' so might experience frustration. In order to build each person's strength and move them to higher levels of faith, God sometimes sent hardships. One suffered but could transcend this suffering by realising that it was all part of God's plan and ultimately things would work out. Individuals might not get the wealth or status that they thought they wanted, but when they understood their place in God's plan they would experience the holistic prosperity that Pastor Vili promised. They also came to see themselves as powerful actors who played an important role in helping the world community. Once people learned to see their lives in terms of this narrative, they, like Pastor Mosese and Sunil, saw blessing in everything that happened to them.

Some people didn't embrace this narrative. I stayed, for instance, with a Fijian man working for the UN and his family in Arusha, Tanzania, who often hosted Harvest Ministry missionaries in East Africa for holidays. The family had recently had a car accident and Pastor Josua, who was staying with them, commented on how blessed the family had been to avoid serious injury. Our host, however, later commented quietly to me that they would have been even more blessed to have not had the accident at all. But those who did come to see their lives as fulfilling a calling in God's world felt important and empowered. And the church community also encouraged people to profess optimism by saying that this was a sign of real faith so those who were most embedded in the church community also found themselves surrounded by narratives of blessing, making it easier for them to see their lives in those terms.

Pastors seldom, if ever, articulated the complete narrative. Instead, they would emphasise some of the elements in particular sermons, leaving the whole narrative to emerge over time. An important step to adopting a positive view of one's life involved learning that one should not expect to be given particular things by God; indeed, often people, like Pastor Mosese, wanted things that would not make them happy. Instead, people should have faith that God would provide. Elenoa, a Fijian missionary in Tanzania, for instance, told me that she found it frustrating that many Tanzanians wanted material rewards from God. 'Seek ye FIRST His kingdom and his righteousness, and all these things will be given to you as well.' 'That means,' she continued, 'that one must have faith in God first, not expect God to prove Himself to you. Once you have that faith, good things will follow.' Similarly, Dr Bob Abramson (2013), an American pastor who was recruited by the Harvest Ministry to train its pastors during the early years of the church, recounts teaching his Fijian pupils that they should have faith in God no matter what happened. He opened each day of an open-air crusade by declaring that God would stop the rain, even though he knew this was unlikely to happen in rainy Suva. When it continued to pour rain every day despite his declarations, he told his assembled students:

> It is not about results or consequences. It is simply about believing
> God is who He says He is and can always do what He says He can
> do. It is about living a life of faith regardless of the consequences
> … We are to believe God without Him having to prove anything
> … Faith is not about results. It is about unwavering trust in God.
> (Abramson 2013, 123–24)

Another important step was to understand that suffering might be
a necessary step in developing faith and becoming stronger. Suffering
brought people to a higher state of faith and fulfilment, although this
higher state did not necessarily involve the individual getting what he or she
had initially wanted. Pastor Anare, for instance, delivered several sermons
about the role of suffering in God's plan when he was the invited speaker
at a summer camp for Harvest Ministry Fijians in the UK serving in the
armed forces. The British government had recently revealed plans for radical
cutbacks in the armed forces, which had generated a lot of anxiety among
the Fijians who worried that Commonwealth soldiers would be let go before
UK citizens. In this context, Pastor Anare spoke each evening about Biblical
instances where mysterious hardships inflicted by God had been followed
by a dramatic reversal of fortune.

On the first evening of the camp, Pastor Anare spoke of God asking Abraham
to sacrifice his only son Isaac. He walked the congregation through each step
of the story, emphasising the importance of faith by declaring that Abraham
had been cheerful and free of doubt at each step of a long three-day journey
from his home to the place where God had asked him to sacrifice Isaac high
in the mountains. At the climax of the story, when God showed Abraham
a ram stuck in some bushes and told him to sacrifice the ram instead of
Isaac, Pastor Anare paused dramatically and asked the congregation if they
had ever wondered about how the ram got to that place. Rams, he said (not
entirely accurately), did not live in high mountains. For the ram to arrive at
that spot at the same time as Isaac and Abraham, God must have sent it to
climb up the mountain just as Abraham and Isaac started up the other side.
When God created a problem, Pastor Anare said, he created the solution
to that problem at the same time. Abraham ultimately went on to be the
father of a great nation, because he understood that God would solve all
the problems he sent. Those who maintained a positive attitude in the face
of adversity, in short, showed their faith in God who would make sure all
problems were solved in the end.

Pastor Anare drew parallels with his own life by telling a story about when he had seemingly insurmountable problems but had maintained faith and the problems been miraculously resolved. He had been travelling to Thailand where he had been asked to take a new job as a regional coordinator with Every Home for Christ. He arrived at the airport in Fiji only to find that the airline had no record of his reservation. He insisted to the people at the check-in desk that he would come back in five minutes and they would then find his reservation in the system. When he returned five minutes later his reservation popped onto the computer screen just as the woman at the counter was about the assure him that he had no ticket. On the same trip, he had to get a Thai visa in Australia but arrived to find that the Thai embassy was closed for a holiday, making it impossible for him to hand in his visa application the required three business days for processing before his scheduled flight to Thailand. When Pastor Anare returned to the embassy the next day the man in charge told him that getting a visa in time was impossible and he would have to change his flight. But Pastor Anare persuaded him to fax his application to Thailand and insisted that when he returned in two days the visa would be there. Two days later the visa had not yet arrived, but Pastor Anare persuaded the man in charge to stay an extra half hour after closing time and the visa miraculously arrived. Like Abraham, Pastor Anare implied, he had been faced with an impossible obstacle, but he had maintained faith and God had presented the solution.

On the second evening, Pastor Anare spoke about Job, who endured great suffering despite being favoured by God. Pastor Anare drew parallels to his own life with two stories. He told of an incident where he had had a very clear vision of the house he wanted to live in in Thailand. However, when he went house hunting he found that such a house was well beyond his means. But he persevered—to the great frustration of his real estate agent—until, out of the blue, a house exactly matching his vision was put on the market and the owners miraculously lowered the price on hearing that Pastor Anare was a man of God.

The second incident involved the death of his young son from leukaemia. Pastor Anare told his audience about how he had fasted and prayed for his son to be healed after the child was diagnosed with leukaemia but had not lost faith when his son had died within a week. He spoke of sitting beside his son's bed and realising the end was near. His son had been suffering but became peaceful and Pastor Anare realised he was with God. Pastor Anare had to leave to preach at the church where he delivered a rousing sermon that brought large numbers of people to the altar to give their lives to Christ. He experienced a moment of pure joy after the sermon when he realised that his son was with God and that God had been 'pruning the vine'—that is, Pastor Anare—to make him better able to fulfil his work of winning souls for God's kingdom.

These stories, like the Biblical stories, involved hardships that were ultimately revealed to be part of God's plan. Pastor Anare masterfully juxtaposed stories of miraculous success, the house hunting venture and the story of his visa, which seemed to show that God would provide for all of his needs, with one of apparent failure, the death of his son despite his week of prayer and fasting. By juxtaposing these two stories, and the Biblical stories of Job and of Abraham's willingness to sacrifice Isaac, Pastor Anare made the point that apparent success and apparent failure were very similar. God was using him, as he had used Job and Abraham, for a purpose that would ultimately be revealed and ultimately would be fulfilling. Sometimes, though, one had to go through a long period of suffering before understanding God's plan since God needed his agents to be strong. And God's plan might be altogether different from what one had hoped for. He joked with the congregation in the UK that if one asked for a breakthrough, God would send a wall so that the person would have something to break through.

On a different occasion, at a Sunday service in Suva, Pastor Tomasi made a similar point about difficult situations leading to success. He also emphasised the ways God's plan sometimes departed from secular ideas of success. He drew interesting parallels between his own life and that of the Biblical widow from Zarephath who used her last oil and flour to feed the prophet Elijah but then was miraculously rescued from certain starvation because of her faithfulness to God. Pastor Tomasi compared this incident to his own decision to turn down a prestigious and lucrative offer to work in an Australian bank in order to return to Fiji from a high-level posting in a Papua New Guinea bank to become a pastor at the Harvest Ministry:

> You see the Zarephath lady, the widow from Zarephath. She was just collecting firewood. She knows that her destiny is death. She knew that they were going to die after eating that meal; they were waiting to die. But the difference is, watch this, God has already chosen to bless this lady. That's why he told Elijah the prophet, 'Go to Zarephath, I have commanded a widow to look after you.' What he was saying was this, what God was saying is this, 'Go to Zarephath. I have chosen to bless a widow from Zarephath, hallelujah.' And the Bible says that not only her but her family, you know her family, don't talk about the village, don't talk about the whole the

whole city of Sidon, because God has chosen to bless one person … God has chosen to bless you this morning because he said in his word in Jeremiah 1:5, 'Before you were born,' he said, 'I knew you. I've appointed you. I've called you.' So all of us this morning, we have been chosen. Tell your neighbour, 'You have been chosen.' You could be going through your Zarephath experience, but God has already chosen you. God has already chosen to bless you.

Pastor Tomasi then turned to his own decision to join the Harvest Ministry:

You know when Pastor Vili called me two years ago from Kenya for me to give up my job and come and work with him here in [Suva], my mind was spinning around … I had a good job. I was senior management at a bank and money was not an issue. I had a good lifestyle. I was staying in a five-star accommodation for nine years. I was set up; I was off; I was (long pause) I was going to give all that up to come and I was trying to work out through my small world. But I never knew God has already figured it out for me in his big world. And as I was walking he dropped the word into my heart and he said, 'Son, what makes you think that [the bank] is a better employer than me.' I hopped into my car, went to my wife and said, 'Hey, guess what? I received this word from God!' … You know coming back to Fiji there are casualties. I have to pay rent. There are bills I have to pay. The car you know when I go to the service station, I have to top up my car. I have to pay. So all of those things and cash flow it goes some times to near negative. So whenever my car is on 'E', I always declare, 'That's Enough.' You know for me 'E' is 'Enough'. Hallelujah!

Here Pastor Tomasi made an interesting parallel between a widow who, facing starvation, gave her last food to the prophet Elijah in obedience and faith, and was rewarded with prosperity, and his own situation, where he had been well off and had decided to devote himself to working for the Harvest Ministry and God and had experienced a decline in his standard of living. Through drawing parallels between the two situations, Pastor Tomasi prompted his audience to conclude that material prosperity was unimportant; if one submitted to God's will, God would provide a rewarding and good life and would make sure that one would have what one needed to survive. Being blessed, in short, did not necessarily mean being wealthy.

In a similar vein, Pastor Luke, a Fijian missionary in Manus, Papua New Guinea, used the story of Moses leaving the Egyptian palace to become a slave to make the point that God purposely put people through hard times to test their obedience, and that ultimately being blessed might involve forsaking lavish wealth in order to lead a good life of service to community. God looked for his leaders, Pastor Luke argued, in ugly situations. Pastor Luke drew parallels between the Biblical story of Moses and the life story of Pastor Vili, showing that both had willingly given up a comfortable life to become leaders and then had been tested by God by having to wait for their final victory. Pastor Luke concluded his sermon by talking about how Pastor Vili had had to go through hard times to attain higher vision:

> I remember the founder of [Harvest Ministry] when God spoke to him. [He had a very good job with the Fiji government and was offered a promotion.] It was during that time that he heard the word of God, [for him] to preach the word of God. He resigned from his work … And there was a time when he felt that God told him to go to the next town and there was no bus fare and as he came to the bus station the bus that was ready to go to the next town was there … Finally … he decided, he made a strong decision, *bai em i tok olsem* [and he said], 'Papa God if I'm going to be ashamed in front of the bus driver because of no bus fare *em i no wari bilong mi, em wari bilong yu* [it is not my concern, it is your concern].' And he made a bold stand that he's going to proceed on. He took the first step, second step when [a] lady called from behind, calling as if they have known each other for long. He turned around, he couldn't recognise the lady but the lady called him as if they [knew] each other and … gave Reverend Vili $10 and that was enough for the fare to take him to the next town to come back … I'm talking about ugly, ugly, ugly situations. God normally takes his people to ugly situations as he prepares them to deliver his people. Hallelujah, once again God will hide a deliverer in an ugly situation to get him to where he needs to go.

In this sermon, Pastor Luke pointed to parallels between the life of Moses, who left the palace to live among slaves and then led them to the promised land, and Pastor Vili, who left a good job to become a pastor to deliver Fijians and unreached peoples. Ultimately hardship was just a sign that greatness was to come and, again, ultimately being blessed meant being of service in God's kingdom, not achieving great wealth.

Pastor Inoke, a Fijian missionary, told a similar story of hardship followed by dramatic reversal in a sermon to his Kenyan congregation. He said that, on a recent trip, he had met an Indian businessman who had been despondent after being fired from his job. His prayer group and Pastor Inoke prayed for him, and a developer appeared who wanted to purchase a piece of the man's land at a high price, thus reversing the initial misfortune.

'God doesn't lie,' Pastor Inoke concluded. God wanted for the faithful to prosper and it was only their own fears and doubts that prevented that from happening. He went on to speak of the example of the widow of Zarephath. Her problems were solved because of her demonstration of faith; Pastor Inoke concluded that God was looking for 'empty vessels' in a state of abject poverty to fill with his blessings.

Those who spoke of their lives in positive terms were viewed as having the faith that was necessary to achieve blessings, a view that implicitly suggested that anxiety and doubt showed lack of faith. This meant that people were under some social pressure to profess optimism. Pastor Anare concluded his sermon on the sacrifice of Isaac, for example, by telling the audience that they should not pray to God for things but instead should just go ahead and thank him for what they wanted, as thanking God for things not yet achieved would show complete faith in God's intention to reward the faithful. And God, of course, rewarded those who had faith and expected to be rewarded.

The story of God preparing the faithful for a purpose that was initially unclear to them, produced a number of narrative devices that people applied to their lives to see themselves as blessed. First, people learned to look for signs that their fate was foreordained by God even though they and others failed to perceive it. Often this involved retroactively interpreting situations as involving an initial setback that was miraculously overcome, confirming in peoples' minds that God was acting in their lives and the eventual outcome was meant to be all along. For instance, Mereseini, told me that she and her husband had been frustrated after being passed over when they applied to be missionaries in East Africa. At the annual Harvest Ministry convention, however, where another couple was to be appointed, they had mysteriously dropped out and Mereseini and her husband were told to get ready to be ordained instead. Mereseini and her husband did not have appropriate clothing because they had not expected this honour, but a woman attending the conference tried on a dress she had brought for the occasion and found it didn't fit, so she offered it to Mereseini and it fit perfectly. Then the same thing happened with a suit for Mereseini's husband. The fact that clothes were supplied out of the blue that fit perfectly, and did not fit those who intended to wear them, seemed to indicate that God had planned all along for Mereseini and her husband to be chosen to be ordained as missionaries.

Similarly, when I first met Siteri, another East African missionary, she told me that she and her husband had also been passed up as missionaries to Africa and sent instead to the interior of Fiji, a difficult posting. But she had had a dream in which she saw herself surrounded by very short people and, when she and her husband were eventually selected to go to Africa, she realised that the people in her dream had an amazing resemblance to those that they ultimately served in Africa, indicating that God had intended all along for them to go to Africa.

In these stories, initial setbacks were overcome, and signs such as dreams and donated clothes that fit showed that the eventual outcome was meant to be all along. Setbacks, then, retroactively were shown to be signs of human failure to perceive God's will, or perhaps tests from God designed to strengthen the recipient to play his or her important role in God's kingdom. When people saw the hand of God in their lives in this fashion, it both confirmed in their minds that problems would work out in the end and convinced them that they were valued by God.

Often people exaggerated the obstacles that had been overcome to prove that God must be involved in resolving the situation. For example, when I flew to Nairobi on my first visit to Fijian missionaries in Kenya my suitcase was delayed (a frequent occurrence in international travel). Pastor Inoke, who had come to meet me in Nairobi, had already bought me a bus ticket so that I could accompany him the next day to the town where he and his family lived. He suggested that we visit the airline's offices in town to enquire about my suitcase. Fortunately, my suitcase had been located and was delivered to my hotel in time for me to take the bus with Pastor Inoke the next day. When Pastor Inoke described these events to his congregation the following Sunday, he insisted that God must have intervened to make sure that my suitcase arrived and I got to my final destination. In this and other instances, people exaggerated the unlikely nature of events to see the hand of God in working things out. It was, after all, not very unusual for my suitcase to be delivered a day late. Even if the delay had been longer, I would surely have gone to visit Pastor Inoke since I had flown to Kenya just for that purpose.

Later, in the same visit, I had to change plans suddenly and return to the US, and Pastor Inoke had to cancel a series of arrangements he had made on my behalf. When I returned a couple of months later Pastor Inoke again told his church members that this whole series of events surely indicated that God wanted us to come together: why else would I leave and then come back?

Similarly, people seemed to go out of their way to interpret material success as a sign that God was acting in their lives by exaggerating the obstacles to that success. One young man told me, for instance, about how he had grown up in a squatter settlement and had been ashamed that his friends might find out that his family used a pit toilet. But, after his family loyally supported the church from the beginning, his mother's travel agency had flourished so his family now had a beautiful house. Another woman told me how she and her husband had struggled to find a nice house at a price they could afford until joining the Harvest Ministry and then happened upon a beautiful house near to the church at a reasonable price.

In both instances, the storyteller seemed to be motivated to interpret success as a blessing from God. The teacher, for instance, had a reasonably good income and was looking for houses in a neighbourhood where real estate was not overly expensive. It is also not surprising that a small travel agency might struggle in its early years and later prosper. In fact, people, like Sunil in the example in the previous chapter, were often aware of other possible explanations for their success but chose to see it as a sign of God's blessing because having a positive attitude towards one's life was a sign of faith in God (Coleman 2000; Luhrmann 2012). The good and obedient Christian trusted that the Lord had a just plan for his or her life and exhibited faith by seeing all events, good or bad, as part of God's plan (Harding 2000, 122–24).

Pastor Levy, a Fijian missionary in another part of East Africa, also told me several stories about great coincidences in his life that showed the hand of God in his life. He told me, for instance, that he when he had served as a missionary in Papua New Guinea he had initially had a very hard time because he didn't have very much money. But he had been taken in by a couple who volunteered to pay all his expenses. He later learned that this was because the couple thought they were cursed because one of their ancestors had killed and eaten a Fijian missionary, so they thought they could reverse the curse by sponsoring Pastor Levy. Pastor Levy also told me of an incident when he was riding in a bus in the Papua New Guinea Highlands and armed robbers tried to stop the bus. Women had been weeping, sure they were going to be raped but he had told everyone just to have faith in God and lo and behold the driver had sped up and gone right past the robbers. Pastor Levy said he had later found a bullet embedded in the seat right next to him. In these and other incidents, Pastor Levy, like other storytellers, saw his life in terms of large insurmountable obstacles that had miraculously disappeared when he had gone ahead and done the unthinkable because he had faith in God.

Exaggerating the humbleness of one's beginning state, as Pastor Maka did when he described the Harvest Ministry pastors as simple village boys in order to stress how unlikely their success was, was another common device employed to imply that God must be involved in causing great events to happen. A common variant of this device was to exaggerate the small size of Fiji, as Pastor Vili did in the sermon described in the opening pages, in order to emphasise how miraculous it was that missionaries should come from Fiji. Fiji is, of course, a small country with a population of less than a million. But it is considered relatively large and developed among Pacific Island nations, many of which are smaller and poorer. One speaker at an annual conference, for instance, joked about how whenever he went through immigration in his travels he had to be sure to bring a copy of a world map with him since customs officers had seldom heard of Fiji and might think his passport was fraudulent if he couldn't prove the existence of Fiji. Again, individuals used this device to experience their own life as blessed: it could only be God's hand that would allow simple village boys from a tiny unknown island to go as missionaries all over the world.

Exaggerating one's lack of qualifications so as to show that God must be behind any successes was a similar device that helped people to see themselves as blessed. Sunil, for instance, told me proudly that he was the least educated member of his sibling set, having just finished secondary school while several of his siblings had higher degrees; however, he neglected to add that he had likely not pursued further education because he had been selected by his father to take over the family contracting business. Sunil pointed to the hand of God in his life by saying that his sisters had recently taken to asking him about Christianity because he was the only one in the family to have converted from Hinduism and he was so much more successful than them. Sunil was quite successful, and his contracting business was flourishing, but dwelling on his lack of qualifications allowed him to see his success as a sign that he was blessed. The humbler one's beginnings, Pastor Josua told an East African congregation on another occasion, the more one's success glorified God. Therefore, the properly worshipful person would see him or herself as coming from humble circumstances in order to make the point that he or she had been empowered by God, so emphasising one's humble beginnings was common in sermons and testimony.

The cumulative effect of hearing many such narratives was to reinforce optimism. Sunil and others were encouraged to see their lives as a series of blessings by pastors who said that God only blessed those who showed faith with their optimistic attitude. This message was a powerful one to Fijians and others living outside of their homelands, exposed to strange and sometimes fearful circumstances and sometimes to prejudice. In Arusha, Tanzania, for instance, an international community worked at the United Nations Commission to look into war crimes in the Rwandan genocide. Other expatriates served as managers at large farms owned by multinational corporations. I attended several gatherings at Pentecostal churches and prayer groups with people from the Philippines, other African countries, and a few Americans and heard stories about how they had been blessed by God. A Filipino couple, for instance, told me how after having three daughters the wife had finally become pregnant with a boy. But early in her pregnancy one of her daughters had gotten the measles and the doctors had insisted that she should abort her baby since he could be born blind or with other disabilities. But the couple had prayed with their Pentecostal prayer group and had decided to keep the baby who had been born healthy with no disabilities. The husband, who worked with the United Nations, told me one evening that it was essential to be a strong Christian when working in such an environment. He told me about backstabbing in the office involving a co-worker who had tried to damage his reputation and take his job. But God had blessed him and the co-worker had been exposed. A Malaysian, serving as senior manager of a flower farm run by a multinational corporation, similarly stressed that God was necessary to success in an alien environment. He said that before he had taken over as manager the farm had not been profitable because of local witchcraft and because employees stole from the company at every opportunity. But after he had taken over he had regularly prayed with his Pentecostal prayer group and had managed to defeat the witchcraft and to stop employees from stealing.

In these and other stories, people cast their lives in terms of a narrative of initial adversity transcended with the aid of God. In the process they learned to see themselves as blessed by God and able to cope in a new and fearful environment.

Gifts and Agency

Pastors also encouraged people to give money to the church by saying that sacrificial giving showed faith that God would provide and by telling people that their ability to give made them powerful actors in the world community (Coleman 2004, 2006). Many Pentecostal churches say that giving shows a willingness to look at the world through 'spiritual' rather than 'physical' eyes and to trust that God has a plan and will provide even if people give away their last dollar (Harding 2000). Giving, as I also heard frequently in East Africa where many people were much poorer than in urban Fiji, also showed a willingness to believe that one, and whatever little one had to give, was of use to the Lord and important. In Fiji, people only occasionally said that giving to the church would bring material blessings from God. Harvest Ministry pastors, like Pastor Tomasi, more commonly talked about how giving to the church helped one to realise one's true role as a powerful actor in a world community.

At the gathering in the UK of Fijians serving in the British Army who belonged to the Harvest Ministry, Pastor Anare emphasised that sacrificial giving without hesitation expressed a willingness to submit to God and created the faith it was supposed to demonstrate. Faith would then help people to weather hard times in the knowledge that God ultimately intended them to lead good lives. In the sermon on God's instructions to Abraham to sacrifice his only son Isaac, Pastor Anare repeatedly stressed Abraham's complete willingness of give sacrificially to God, describing in detail how difficult it had been for a father to sacrifice an only son, one who was born to him in old age. Focusing on a verse in which Abraham told his servants to wait with the donkeys at the foot of the mountain while Abraham took Isaac to the place of sacrifice, Pastor Anare drew attention to Abraham's parting words to his servants:

> He said, 'WE will go and worship, WE will go up together, my son and me, WE will come down together.' He didn't say, 'We will go up and worship and I will come down.' He said, 'We will go up to worship and WE will come down together.' What a declaration of faith! Abraham knew even if he had to kill sacrifice his son on the altar, somehow God would overcome! (huge applause) … When he declared [it], God was pleased and God said, 'I've never seen faith like that.' He declared, 'WE are going up together and WE are coming down together.' Hallelujah! (Hallelujah) WHAT A FAITH!!!

Abraham, Pastor Anare declared, was clearly confident that if he was willing to give all to God, God would provide for him, in this case by allowing him to keep Isaac. His very willingness to give allowed him to endure the hardship of being asked to sacrifice his son. When people gave willingly, this made them overcomers demonstrating their faith in God, willing to walk out in faith and power and to act on the world (see also Harding 2000, 122–24).

This sense of empowerment helped Fijians in the UK. At the UK gathering, people spoke of feeling isolated and having marital problems owing to the lack of extended family and community support. For instance, one man told me how wonderful it was to be with other Fijians at the camp, as, ordinarily, he and others lived in housing developments where neighbours did not know each other and did not help each other, as was typical of people in the UK. If someone died or was sick, the neighbours would never know. People also spoke of facing prejudice in the UK, noting, for instance, that soldiers from the Commonwealth generally were passed over for the best jobs and assigned the most dangerous duties. Giving, then, was not a means to attain wealth but instead was a way of becoming a valued person in a world community and of increasing confidence that one was important in God's kingdom (see also Premawardhana 2012).

Giving also created the feelings of confidence that it was meant to express. Pastor Vili, for instance, recounted on more than one occasion an incident when he had been approached by a man at a conference in the US who felt he lacked in faith and wanted to know how to deepen his belief. Pastor Vili had told the man to get out his chequebook and write a cheque for world mission, since it was God's will to spread the gospel all over the world. When the man asked how much money he should give, Pastor Vili jokingly suggested that he give all that he had, since people's hearts followed their treasure. In short, as I heard other pastors repeat, giving in itself created the right attitude of willingness to submit to God and confidence that God would provide for the faithful, since when you gave money you were then motivated to be concerned about its fate. If you gave all your money to world mission, you would surely then develop faith that world mission was important.

Harvest Ministry sermons also created agency by emphasising that giving made Fijians important actors in a world community. For instance, at the 2012 annual conference in Suva, one of the Fijian pastors opened the evening with the standard call for offerings that would support world mission, which was highlighted at the conference where Fijian missionaries were brought home to talk about their work. Pastor Maka started by reading the story of the widow of Zarephath. Pastor Maka commented that surely the widow was in this bad condition to start with because she had a 'weak anointing', and that by connecting herself to the Lord she was connecting herself to a strong anointing just as the congregation would connect themselves to 'something bigger' than themselves when they gave to world mission. Giving empowered people by placing them squarely within a world community of Christians.

The global anointing, however, was seldom portrayed as bringing material prosperity to Fiji. Indeed, Harvest Ministry pastors often reminded people in Fiji that they already were prosperous compared to people in many areas of the world. This was a particularly common theme in Suva, where pastors told the relatively affluent urban congregation that they had benefited materially and spiritually when the British had brought Christianity to Fiji and it was now their obligation to help those who 'followed behind'. Pastor Vili spoke on other occasions of how poor the 'unreached peoples' groups' to whom the Harvest Ministry sent missionaries were in comparison to Fijians:

> Those unreached peoples groups they are the poorest among the poorest, the neglected among the neglected and the forsaken among the forgotten … Why should the people hear the gospel twice when billions of people have never heard their first gospel message? I really believe we need to be thinking of people who are still on the back row still waiting to receive their first gospel message. The churches they have built, that's the first Christian churches that's ever been built among these unreached people's groups since Jesus gave the Great Commission. Those are the first-generation Christians.

A similar message was delivered by Ulf Ekman, of the Swedish Word of Life Church, at an annual Harvest Ministry conference in Fiji. Here it was clear that Fijians had joined Euro-Americans as mission senders, ready to convert prosperity into agency on a world scale. Ulf Ekman reminded the Fijian congregation that participation in a world Christian community would bring personal fulfilment beyond what could be realised through material wealth, implying that he was speaking to an audience that had already realised sufficient prosperity, like his Swedish congregation back home, and could now move on building a satisfying life:

> You are not a consumer of a spiritual experiences. By the Holy Spirit you are a producer of spiritual life ... But you are not blessed just to get a television and a better car; you are blessed to produce life all over the world. You are blessed to break through barriers ... To live for yourself is to be lonely! To live for yourself is to be locked into something that you cannot escape from! Is to live in bondage! Your gifts, the operations in your life cannot come out into freedom! Your talents are wasted! Your life, your time is wasted! ... We are alive for a purpose. And the purpose is not me ... I belong to the body of Christ. Praise God. I'm never alone anymore.

Ekman went on to praise the Fijians for going out as missionaries to Rwanda, referring to the opening of that night, when Fijian missionaries from East Africa had appeared to talk about their work. Implicit was the idea that Fijians were similar to Euro-American Christians, already prosperous and, as such, were poised to contribute to a world community of Christians. 'Blessing', as Pastor Vili often reminded his congregation, was not just financial prosperity but a more holistic spiritual, social, physical and emotional prosperity, which both followed on and enabled one to play one's role in building God's kingdom on earth.

Conclusion

Harvest Ministry members learned to see themselves as blessed and as powerful agents in a world community. At the same time, they were prompted to think that though people often wanted material things, God had plans for them that might take them in other directions and would ultimately be more satisfying. Sermons and personal testimony encouraged people to have faith and a positive attitude and to see both good and bad things in their lives as part of God's plan. In Fiji, Harvest Ministry pastors convinced relatively affluent urban professionals that they were already prosperous and were poised to be major contributors to a world community. As I will show in following chapters, in East Africa and Papua New Guinea, pastors with less prosperous congregations nevertheless resisted the idea that they were receivers and encouraged congregations that those who gave were asserting faith in God.

6

Mission from 'Everywhere to Everywhere': Imagining Mission from the Global South

Anderson (2013), Jenkins (2006), Sanneh (2003) and others suggest that partnerships between churches in the global south might produce a Christianity informed by experiences of powerlessness. These views are echoed by some mainstream North American and Western European churches who look to mission from 'everywhere to everywhere' to break the former association between colonialism and missionisation. For example, the Common Call of the Edinburgh 2010 World Missionary Conference outlined a vision for world mission produced by the assembled representatives from Catholic, Evangelical, Orthodox, Pentecostal and Protestant churches from all over the world. The conference was 'mindful of the shift in the centre of gravity of world Christianity to the global south' (Kim and Anderson 2011, 4), and challenged Christians to acknowledge and address the 'asymmetries and imbalances of power' and to be accountable in their 'use of power structures' (Kim and Anderson 2011, 1). As one keynote speaker argued, the paradigm of world mission had shifted over the past century and people were looking for ways to divorce mission from Euro-American colonialism and neocolonialism and to empower voices from all over the world to contribute to dialogues on world Christianity. Mission should involve Christians going from 'everywhere to everywhere' to foster renewal and critical thought (Robert 2011).

However, ethnographic studies of mission-sending churches from the global south, such as the Brazilian Universal Church of the Kingdom of God, reveal that, while south–south mission produces different dynamics than mission from centre to periphery, it does not necessarily contest sources of global inequality. In fact, some churches embrace the same stereotypes and ideas as Euro-American organisations with whom they have worked.

In this chapter, I analyse Harvest Ministry views of mission as presented in Suva, and then in the next two chapters show how the views of Fijian missionaries change when they encounter the mission field. In a nutshell, I suggest that Fijian and Papua New Guinean views of mission mirror those of the American parachurch organisation Every Home for Christ, for whom the Pacific Islanders had originally worked. Pacific Islanders generally endorsed ideas of unilineal development reminiscent of modernisation theory from the 1950s and created an imagined world community peopled by various stock characters drawn out of Euro-American Pentecostal literature. In Suva conferences where the church solicited donations to support world mission and other causes, Pacific Islanders were portrayed as a spiritual but economically developed vanguard poised between the unreached peoples and the wealthy nations of North America, Europe and the Far East. The unreached had simple, childlike faith but were oppressed by senior male 'witchdoctors' and wealthier people in the same nation. Europeans, North Americans and many Asians were wealthy but spiritually dead. All of these groups were deeply grateful when they were rescued by Pacific Island missionaries. These views had obvious fundraising benefits.

Pacific Island missionaries carried these views into their mission fields where they met so-called unreached peoples who had already received the gospel and did not particularly want to be rescued by Fijians. Sometimes missionaries changed their views. But they also sometimes concluded that they had yet to contact the unreached and had been waylaid by intermediary groups who themselves exploited the unreached. While missionaries from the global south did not bring significantly different ideas to world Christianity than their Euro-American counterparts, they did end up influencing each other's views and creating a genuine dialogue between Christians from different backgrounds simply because their relative lack of money and power led to a situation where no one could impose his ideas on others.

Mission from the Best to the Rest: The View from Suva

I am sitting in the Suva church in May 2012 and the huge auditorium is packed to capacity with people from Fiji, Papua New Guinea, Australia and New Zealand, and a smattering of guests from other parts of the world, many of them Fijians living abroad who have returned for the annual Harvest Ministry conference. It is early May and Suva is hot and humid. The auditorium is poorly ventilated and packed full of people who have been singing and dancing vigorously. The heat is so oppressive that I am covered with sweat and feel a bit faint. The lights dim and a spotlight dramatically casts a map of the Fiji Islands on the floor. A voice narrates over the auditorium loudspeaker as music begins to play and the youth dance team appears on the stairways radiating up from the main floor:

> In the year 1990 a vision was birthed … through the man of God, Reverend Viliame Lagilagi, President of the Harvest Ministry International. God called him to bear the hardship, bring back the lost and to train and equip believers for the Great Commission … On September 18, 1992, Reverend Viliame was made president of the Harvest Ministry … In the year 2002 our first missionary, Pastor Josua, was sent to Tanzania. We are now able to build a bridge to the second largest continent of the world. Ladies and gentlemen we bring you Africa … To the nation of Tanzania and its Maasai tribe, the love of God for this tribe opens the pathway for Harvest Ministry to give them their first taste of clean water. Our missionary to the nation has also been drilling boreholes for fresh and clean water and has built 25 permanent church buildings … They've also established farming projects in Tanzania. We are so privileged to have access to so much clean water [here in Fiji]; if only we would know the value of just one drop [to those who do not have a regular supply of clean water]. We now shift our focus to the Batwa Pygmy people of Rwanda. With a history of civil war and acts of genocide these people have always faced the sheer reality of improper housing, let alone proper sanitation. The Harvest Ministry has been consistent in adhering to the cry of this nation by seeing to the building of homes for this unique tribe. According to [our] missionary sent to the nation of Rwanda, they have recently built 23 homes for the Pygmy people. To the nation of Kenya we introduce you to the Turkana tribe. In this nation, education, schools, are a pressing need for the children. The Harvest Ministry International strongly believes in proper education; this was yet another opportunity to spread Jesus

to the lives of these children despite the lack of opportunities. Just seeing these children learning is worth every penny of investment. [Our missionary] has also built a borehole for fresh clean water in Kenya where a woman was able to have her first taste of clean fresh water at the age of 70. The two-hand gospel was demonstrated through the building of churches, schools and homes among the unreached peoples' groups in Kenya, Uganda, Madagascar, Tanzania and Rwanda. Ladies and gentlemen these were all made possible through your prayers and generous giving!

The next item is a lively dance in which dozens of Fijian teenagers dressed in faux-African head scarves and colourful costumes dance to Kiswahili hymns and act out a skit involving village women pumping fresh water from a new borehole and distributing it to happy villagers. Then the house lights are turned up and Pastor Tomasi, the director of the World Mission department, takes the stage draped in a colourful Maasai blanket. Pastor Tomasi takes the microphone and calls out:

> Hallelujah! Awesome! Amen! Awesome! This is our story. This is our song. This is our DNA. This is who we are. Just the joy of sowing into the mission field and just the joy of seeing the mission reaching people who have never heard the gospel once in their lifetime, amen? … I shall now call upon Pastor Josua … He will pray in Swahili, amen, and we may not understand what he is saying but I pray that we all support him, amen, as he stands on our behalf and prays. Amen?

Pastor Josua prays in rapid and fluent Kiswahili for about three minutes and then is joined on stage by Pastor Vili who invites the Fijian and Papua New Guinean missionaries posted in East Africa and their families to take the stage. These families have come to Fiji for six months to appear at Harvest Ministry churches around the country to talk about their work and to raise funds to support their missions. Pastor Vili assures the congregation that every penny they give will go directly to world mission and none will be absorbed in the church bureaucracy. Pastor Vili interviews the families one by one, starting with Pastor Josua and family. After talking briefly to the children, Pastor Vili asks Pastor Josua to tell the audience about Jeremy, a young Maasai man whose sister was promised in marriage to an elder who already had several wives. Pastor Josua tells the story of Jeremy and the 'witchdoctor' or *laiboni* who wanted to marry Jeremy's sister who was only in eighth grade. Jeremy reported the *laiboni* to the police, even though the *laiboni* threatened to bewitch and kill him. When the *laiboni* was released from jail he cast a spell on Jeremy, but Josua prayed and fasted with him. Josua concludes:

> Until today, Jeremy is still alive! Hallelujah! … You know the problem about Maasai people they don't read; they don't write; they believe the message that you say but to take out the message that was already there from their great grandfather or from their grandfather, it's very hard, just like some Fijians! (laughter) … When that thing happened when they realised that Jeremy didn't die after three days, they said, 'Ha, ha so Jeremy's God is much, much greater than *laiboni*'s God.' So everywhere we go, every village we enter, definitely people they change and they pray and they believe God and today almost every village we enter we must plant a church because people are there, they believe that Jeremy's God is much, much greater than *laiboni*'s God (applause).

Pastor Vili then moves on to a Fijian couple, Na Lela (Mother Lela) and Pastor Tevita, working as missionaries among the Batwa 'Pygmies' of Rwanda. The couple describes how the Batwa have been pushed by their fellow countrymen into marginal land where they live in temporary shelters made of leaves, are short of food and lack water for washing. Pastor Tevita describes how they built a house for a pregnant woman who was deeply grateful to have a shelter over her head before her baby was born. Na Lela concludes their testimony:

> One day when we went up [to where the Batwa live] they were all cleaning something and I looked in the basin I saw some green little stuff. They were removing the legs and the wings and that day people were going to eat grasshoppers for a meal. So I joined them in the kitchen and we cooked and we had grasshopper for a meal (laughter) and I want to tell you today that grasshopper is really delicious; more delicious, it tastes better than prawn that we eat here (laughter). So those people they really live according to God's word: do not worry about tomorrow for tomorrow will take care of itself. I challenge you today you know you can plant a seed to clothe those who have no clothes, to feed those who have no food, to send those children to school. May God bless you.

The other missionaries tell stories of bringing solar-powered audio Bibles to people deep in the rainforest who had never heard of Jesus and of digging wells for African pastoralists who had never before tasted clean water and cried in gratitude.

These stories portrayed the unreached peoples of Africa in terms of a stock set of stereotypes. Some, like the Maasai described in Pastor Josua's story, were dominated by male elders who exploited young women, kept them from becoming educated and terrorised the population through threats of witchcraft. Such stories kept younger people in line and prevented them from seeking out opportunities that might help them and their communities to progress. Other unreached peoples, like the Batwa Pygmy of Na Lela's story, had a simple, natural spirituality and lived 'according to God's word', knowing 'not to worry about tomorrow for tomorrow [would] take care of itself'. The Batwa and others, however, were neglected, downtrodden victims of their own countrymen living in dire poverty.

The unreached were always portrayed, as in Pastor Josua's and Pastor Tevita's stories, as deeply grateful when Fijian missionaries liberated them from oppressive elders and brought the benefits of education. These themes were particularly prominent on that Africa night in 2012 when Pastor Inoke spoke of how he and his Papua New Guinean assistant had initially encountered resistance among a group of Kenyan pastoralists, but had won the group over through showing them that people had come all the way from Fiji to help them when people in their own nation would not. Pastor Inoke described the opening of a new well. The well had been built by World Vision, but Pastor Inoke suggested that World Vision had only noticed this group because the Harvest Ministry was working there. Pastor Inoke described the scene:

> Just imagine right now the temperature [there] it's almost 40 [centigrade]. You know it's very hot and we thank God for the first time we provide water and we pray so that God may able to, you know, right now we have a borehole you know on the 23rd of December … Right now they are drinking fresh water and I still remember the first time we went and then we provided water there was a lady, who she was 72 years old and tears was coming to her face and she was trying to express herself using her own language and I knew she was trying to tell me something and I asked my interpreter, 'What's happening?' and my interpreter said, 'You know Pastor, you know what she is trying to tell you? Since she was young till now, 70 years old, she never tasted a pure water. But because you came she has tasted pure water' (applause).

Pastor Inoke went on to describe their efforts to introduce schools. He said the people had initially resisted the idea because they wanted their children to herd animals, but that the Fijian team had prayed and fasted and then eventually some families had agreed to send their children to school. A local teacher commented: 'Eh the missionaries from Fiji they are working right to our people.' Pastor Inoke said the teacher had told them:

> 'Pastor if you can come right from Fiji to pastor to my people I am willing and I volunteer to teach these children' ... You know one thing I was really amazed and it really touched me, when we took the first step we saw the people they have the confidence, they just came and say, 'We can do this'. They collected stones and also the soil, you know, everything, you know. I see it just gave them a confidence because this is what they said, 'You know the government it rejected us, just imagine you come right from Fiji and we thank God we knew that somebody cares for us'.

Pastor Inoke went on to say that oil reserves had been discovered under this tribe's land and that the local people had suggested that he was responsible for this blessing because he had brought them to God's attention:

> I still remember when a man came and he said, 'Pastor you know the church has done a lot of things and a lot of impact in this place but because of what you have been doing now we've found the biggest oil in the whole world even though you know oil has been found in the Sudan and also in Ethiopia. But the biggest oil that has been found it's right on the very spot that we have begun the work'. And the man came and he said, 'Pastor because we began something; that's why all the things that were hidden it's coming up'.

Here Pastor Inoke evoked images of an oppressed people living without technology in a harsh desert environment who were deeply grateful that Fijians would help them when their own countrymen failed to do so. When Fijian missionaries provided clean water and built schools, people cried in gratitude and gained the confidence to volunteer their own time and labour to the school. When these neglected people were brought to God's attention by Fijian missionaries, he continued to bless them by revealing oil reserves beneath their land.

Similar images were used to describe the unreached in other areas of the world in that 2012 convention and in less formal conversations I had with Harvest Ministry missionaries. Another night of the 2012 Suva convention featured presentations from Papua New Guineans working with the Harvest Ministry in Papua New Guinea and the Solomon Islands. They told stories of crossing rivers and climbing through dense rainforest for six hours beyond the end of roads to reach people who had never seen clothes before, and to convert an elderly chief among the Kwaio of the Solomon Islands who had lived his days without hearing of the Bible. Another Papua New Guinean pastor told of his efforts to reach a very remote group:

> The people when they first wore the clothes they did not know whether these clothes are for male or these clothes are for female so the boys just have to wear the clothes for the ladies … and also if they want to cover their body in the night they use this mosquito net that we sent to cover them (laughter). They do not know whether this one is for protection for the mosquito or they just wear it … I can still remember one man I brought him down to the town and that one he never drove in the car so and so we were trying to teach him how to sit on the bus and he was trying to jump out of the window (laughter).

Another member of the Papua New Guinean delegation described a group who lived in trees and still had tails living near the border between Papua New Guinea and Indonesia:

> On the Indonesian border there is a group there, a group of people that have tails … and we really want to reach out to them. We really want to make a difference among that group and in June this year we have already trained a group that is going across to that place … We have already mobilised them they are now ready to go and it is our goal it is our heart to really do something that is going to bring this group out although they are disliked but we want to do something that is going to really make a difference in their lives.

In these and other stories, the unreached peoples of various areas of the world were described as living in such a 'primitive' and isolated state that they resembled animals and had a childlike wonder at modern technology.

Similar themes were also present in the stories that Pacific Islanders told me when I visited East Africa. Siteri, who worked with her husband in Madagascar, spoke warmly of how hardworking and enterprising the unreached peoples' group they served were and how they used simple hand-operated machines to crush sugar and mill rice. Yet, despite their work, they were very poor, perhaps because of the prevalence of witchcraft, which prevented them from developing.

Fijian missionaries also thought that the Africans they served were amazed by the wonders of civilisation. For instance, Siteri said she had really enjoyed the times that people from the remote areas had come to town to stay with them. One woman had been so awed by the shower that she used an entire bar of soap standing there. Afterwards she just stood on the towel Siteri had provided because she didn't know how to use it to dry herself. Her children, Siteri said, were always setting aside toys and clothes to send to the unreached peoples. Once, her eight-year-old son had gone to visit the unreached with his father and had healed a young boy there by laying on hands.

Harvest Ministry missionaries, like Pastor Josua at the convention, also spoke of women as being oppressed and lacking access to education. When I accompanied Mereseini, who served with her husband in Kenya, on her first visit to the tribal group they were assigned to reach further north in Kenya, she particularly wanted to speak to the women. The Harvest Ministry was building a school in one area and Mereseini told the assembled students that it was very important, particularly for girls, to complete school. She told them that she had wanted to be an aeroplane pilot when she was a child. Although she had not achieved this goal, she had become a missionary who had left Fiji to come all the way to Africa. They too should have dreams and should become educated to achieve their goals. She later told me that she was distressed that families in this group withdrew girls from school and married them off to older men when they were only 12 or 13. Again, these stories feature women and younger men who are powerless in the face of male elders. Those receiving the gospel would be grateful to their liberators.

An International Hierarchy of Stereotypes

The views presented at the Suva conference and by missionaries were clearly drawn from a set of stereotypes shared by other groups who differed largely on the place to which they assigned their own group in the hierarchy. Harvest Ministry ideas about naturally spiritual, childlike 'primitives' oppressed by evil spirits and witchdoctors clearly borrowed from Every Home for Christ, the American church organisation for whom Pastor Vili and many of the Harvest Ministry missionaries had worked before the founding of the Harvest Ministry. Dick Eastman, international president of Every Home for Christ, wrote in his book, *Beyond Imagination*, of several instances in which missionaries had come to the aid of young people, particularly women, who were oppressed by elders and males. One story told of a young woman in the Philippines who was able to free herself from an abusive husband after tricking him into taking a Bible course with her (Eastman 1997, 185–86). Another told of a young Muslim woman in North Africa whose family attempted to execute her using a homemade electric chair when she expressed interest in Christianity. After escaping and fleeing naked to the home of some Christian friends, she was ultimately protected by the Holy Spirit who clothed her in a white gown. Another story told of a young Hindu man suffering from pain, dizziness and loss of appetite. His parents blamed his young wife for bringing the wrath of evil spirits upon them and drove the young couple and their baby out to live in a cow shed. The young couple were instructed by an exploitative witchdoctor to make so many sacrifices that eventually they decided to kill themselves and their two children. But they were miraculously saved after leaping into a raging river and then helped by a Christian doctor who taught them about the Bible and liberated them from oppressive spirits and relatives (Eastman 1997, 33–34).

Eastman portrays people as being amazed when exposed to the material culture of the outside world. People such as the Kwaio of the Solomon Islands are described as living deep in the mountains and being only vaguely aware of such dramatic events as World War II, even when bombs were exploding around them. Eastman describes the life of an old chief and priest, Haribo, who lived for over 100 years before he became aware of the outside world. When Haribo was almost 90 years old, he and his fellow villagers wondered about some 'brilliant shooting stars streaking across the ink-black Pacific sky'. Haribo explained to his fellow villagers that these stars—in reality, missiles in World War II—'were reminders that ancestral spirits are near' (Eastman 1997, 139). Later, Haribo sacrificed pigs and chickens to save his fellow villagers from an epidemic, but 'sometimes he dreamed of a peaceful place with no pain or suffering, but he had no idea how to find that place' (Eastman 1997, 121).

Eastman portrays groups such as the Kwaio as having a natural spirituality. When two Every Home for Christ missionaries finally penetrated to Haribo's village to deliver the gospel message to his deathbed, Haribo told them:

> I have waited my entire lifetime to hear this story … I have always felt there was some sacred message like this. But no one ever came to bring us such words. How can I receive this Jesus into my life? (Eastman 1997, 228)

Eastman similarly describes the Pygmies of the central African rainforest as naturally spiritual but oppressed by evil spirits:

Witchcraft and black magic permeate all aspects of life. These 'people of the trees' believe their high death rate from malaria and other diseases is actually caused by black magic or evil spirits. (Eastman 1997, 155)

But, like Haribo, the Kwaio priest, Lendongo, a young Pygmy chief, has a natural spirituality and suspects that there is a better life. Eventually, Every Home for Christ workers penetrate the jungles of Zaire in canoes to find the Pygmies living in trees and manage to convert them and deliver them from the Ebola virus through the power of prayer.

Pacific Islander views also resembled those of Euro-American Christian organisation such as World Vision. Bornstein (2005, 46) says that workers in North American Christian non-government organisations (NGOs), such as World Vision in Zambia, divide the world into those who are and are not 'reached' by the gospel of Jesus and assume that the 'unreached' are also 'undeveloped'. Receiving the gospel will empower people to plan their own way to development, and learning good Christian habits will help people to prosper. These organisations, however, see their work as helping people to define their own desires and plan their own projects. Speakers in Harvest Ministry conventions in Suva, on the other hand, conveyed a clear sense of knowing what the unreached needed to learn.

Similar ideas about an international hierarchy of knowledge and spirituality were expressed by people in other churches and by speakers at the Suva convention. For instance, when I talked to a Catholic priest from the Philippines stationed in a coastal area of Papua New Guinea, he described Papua New Guineans in the area in similar terms to those used by the Pacific Island missionaries to describe Africans and more remote New Guineans. The priest said that Catholicism in Papua New Guinea was very unsophisticated compared to the Philippines where the Catholic Church had arrived some 450 years ago, but that the Papua New Guineans had a very simple, natural capacity for faith that was helped along by the absence of exposure to the distractions of mass media. Likewise, at one conference at the Harvest Ministry in Suva, the wife of a visiting pastor from New Zealand spoke of her husband's first visit to Fiji to an outer island where the people had gathered in a church building with a dirt floor and had been 'covered in dust but full of the joy of the Lord'.

In short, Fijians, Papua New Guineans, Filipinos, New Zealanders and Euro-Americans drew on a common stock of essentialised stereotypes. Papua New Guineans and Fijians, who were themselves considered primitive, simple and childlike by Euro-Americans, used such stereotypes to describe Africans and Pacific Islanders living in more remote locations. They took pride in showing that they had moved on from the state of their ancestors and were now ready to join Euro-Americans in spreading the benefits of civilisation to others (see also Ryle 2010).

Spiritually Dead Wealthy Nations

On the other end of the spectrum were the materially prosperous but spiritually dead people living in industrialised nations of the world. At the 2012 Suva convention, the third night was 'European night'. The presentation started with a video praising the British for bringing Christianity to Fiji in 1835 and noting that Fijians themselves had gone as missionaries to Papua New Guinea just 40 years later. Since 1999, the video narrative continued, Fijians belonging to the Harvest Ministry had been serving with the British armed forces where they worked within the army to establish Bible study groups and to bridge racial barriers. Pastor Tomasi, this time wearing a shirt with a Union Jack pattern, invited Pastor Semesi, who was stationed in the UK to serve Fijians in the British military, to talk about his work.

Pastor Semesi began by commenting that there had been a rise in 'witchcraft and Islam in UK'. But, after four years of midnight prayers by every Fijian soldier, God had begun to move. Pastor Semesi launched into a humorous account of picking up a young British man who was hitchhiking after attending a big gathering of 'witchcraft people'. Pastor Semesi told the young man:

> You hopped in the right car tonight! We are Fijians! We were cannibals! We found out that white blood is so tasty! Fijians drink blood and eat human flesh. Now we are after your soul.

Pastor Semesi joked that they had continued on right past their turnoff to take their hitchhiker to his destination, talking to him about God and the Bible and that when they had dropped the young man off he said: 'Thank God for those Fijians!' This story again alluded to essentialised images of Fijians as primitive savages who had received Christianity from the British but had now reversed roles and were bringing Christianity to British youth who were dabbling in witchcraft. Such images create pride in middle-class Fijians by placing them at the forefront of a world community of Christians. The appeal of such images for fundraising is obvious.

I heard stories about the lack of spirituality in industrialised nations in East Africa where one of the bishops working with the Harvest Ministry started his regional conference by talking about a recent trip to Japan. The Japanese, he said, worked amazingly hard. They would not waste time on a long aeroplane trip as an African would but instead sat working on their laptops the whole time. But they were lonely and suicide rates were high. They needed the gospel to bring meaning to their lives.

Conclusion

The Edinburgh 2010 Common Call on world mission suggests empowering voices from the 'majority world' or global south to promote a genuine dialogue on Christianity and a questioning of economic and political inequalities. Fijians, East Africans and Papua New Guineans embraced the view that they had a special place in world Christianity, and this was an empowering image of them. It is not always apparent, though, that mission from the Pacific promoted different views or questioning of inequality.

In the next two chapters I examine the Harvest Ministry in East Africa and Papua New Guinea to argue that Fijians and Papua New Guineans who served as missionaries in Africa developed more nuanced views but still retained some of the same beliefs. The situation of collaborating as relative equals did eventually promote a kind of dialogue that might not have occurred if one side had been a great deal wealthier and more powerful than the other.

7

Connecting to a Vision: Harvest Ministry in Papua New Guinea

It is a rainy day in Alotau, capital of Milne Bay Province, Papua New Guinea, where I have come to visit the Harvest Ministry. Nothing much is going on with the small local Harvest Ministry congregation of 19 adults and 23 children, so I have decided to spend the day visiting other churches to ask them if they send missionaries overseas and what they think of the Harvest Ministry. I happen upon Jonas, a friendly and talkative Papua New Guinean pastor working with a Pentecostal church originally started by Scandinavian missionaries, now under local leadership with several branches in Milne Bay Province. Jonas, happy to pass the time on a slow day talking to an American anthropologist, has never heard of the Harvest Ministry and had never met Pastor Maciu, the Fijian missionary who lived in the small town of Alotau (population 16,000) for seven years before being called back to Fiji just a few months earlier. Jonas seems, moreover, to be slightly puzzled about the concept of Fijian missionaries in Milne Bay Province. Papua New Guineans, he notes, are really grateful to the Fijian missionaries who worked with the London Missionary Society and were among the first to bring Christianity to Milne Bay in the late nineteenth century. But now Milne Bay Province has so many churches that they compete with each other for resources and congregation members. In fact, he says, he has been thinking recently that it would be much better if all the churches just got together and worked cooperatively since they all preach similar messages.

Why, he wonders, would Fijians want to come now and start yet another church and undercut the good work started by their own ancestors over a century ago?

When I ask whether Jonah's church sends missionaries from Papua New Guinea to other areas, Pastor Jonas perks up. He himself started with the United Church but was recruited by Youth with a Mission, a North American organisation, when he was attending university in Port Moresby, and travelled all around the country with them participating in crusades before being sent to a Bible college in Australia for a year and a half. After Bible school, Jonas was posted on one of the many islands in Milne Bay Province. But then Youth with a Mission sent him to a discipleship school in Hawaii for three months and then on three missions: Japan, the Olympics in Los Angeles and India. Jonas said that he did really well in India, much better than the Americans and Canadians working there; people had thought he was Indian because of the way he looked. But he got sick and had to come home. He was supposed to go to Africa where he had heard that Papua New Guineans were much more successful than Americans as missionaries because they were used to hardship and could live among the locals. North American missionaries, who were used to a higher standard of living, tended to live in towns, remote from the people they served. But the bottom had dropped out of the Papua New Guinean kina and so he had lost his funding and had had to stay home.

Pastor Jonas's remarks captured many of the themes that I found to be central to the Harvest Ministry, Papua New Guinea. First, some individual Fijians, like Pastor Tomasi and Pastor Jone, were very successful and popular pastors in Papua New Guinea. But many other Fijian pastors, such as Pastor Maciu, had small congregations and, as a group, Fijians seemed to enjoy no better connection with Papua New Guineans or success as missionaries than Europeans, Americans and Australians. I visited Fijian missionaries in Manus and Lae and heard about ones who had served in Papua New Guinea for several years and had recently been reassigned back to Fiji in Port Moresby and Alotau. These Fijians had small congregations, often built around one key individual with some connection to Fiji, such a relative in Fiji or a Fijian co-worker. Further, many Papua New Guineans, like Pastor Jonas, thought that Papua New Guinea was beyond the stage of needing missionaries, unless those missionaries brought with them substantial material resources. This was particularly the case in the coastal and island areas like Milne Bay Province, which had been Christian since the late nineteenth century. Most of the Fijian missionaries, however, were located in such areas.

Second, Papua New Guineans, like Pastor Jonas, were familiar with the idea that Papua New Guineans would be good missionaries because they were used to living in humble circumstances and, as fellow 'black skins', would more easily relate to people like Africans or Australian Aboriginal people who might be suspicious of Euro-Americans because they were associated with former colonisers. They had learned these ideas from accounts of nineteenth-century groups such as the London Missionary Society (Tippett 2014; see also Timmer 2012) and from contemporary North American organisations active in Papua New Guinea like Youth with a Mission and Every Home for Christ. The Harvest Ministry was just one more organisation promoting the idea of mission from the global south and many Papua New Guineans had gone on short-term missions to other areas of the world. On the other hand, many were dubious about Fijian missionaries, saying that Fijians often seemed to be 'culturally unable' to humble themselves to live among the people they served.

Christians from the global south, in short, had no special connection with each other and no distinctive shared vision. Each group drew elements from the transnational rhetoric that increased its own sense of connection and agency in an imagined world community. Yet, it was also clear that this community wasn't solely imaginary, since many people, like Pastor Jonas, had been sent by churches for Bible school training and missions in other areas of the world. Being a missionary or a Pentecostal pastor did offer some genuine mobility for a group of people whose chances of connecting to a wider world were objectively limited.

In this chapter, I examine the Harvest Ministry in Papua New Guinea to argue that Fijians had no special connection with Papua New Guineans. In Suva, the Harvest Ministry appealed to successful urban professionals by suggesting that the Fijians would serve as a spiritual vanguard guiding people in other areas of the world towards spiritual and material prosperity. Fijian missionaries in Papua New Guinea, however, encountered Papua New Guineans who saw themselves as spiritual equals. In response, Fijians acted as spiritual leaders only in very circumscribed contexts, such as dealing with youth in squatter settlements, and stressed that their vision did not stem from greater spiritual enlightenment but instead came from their position as outsiders who could see past local conventions.

Papua New Guineans were often suspicious of Fijian missionaries and thought that the key to spreading the word of God was personal humility, a trait they thought was more likely to be found in Papua New Guineans than

Fijians. Those who liked the Harvest Ministry were attracted to the fact that it seemed to offer youth manageable steps towards connecting with a wider world. Papua New Guineans also liked the idea that they were superior missionaries.

Harvest Ministry Papua New Guinea

The largest Harvest Ministry congregations in Papua New Guinea were in the Autonomous Region of Bougainville, formerly a province of Papua New Guinea that had attained the status of an autonomous zone after a protracted civil war (1988–98). Pastor Isaiah, the senior pastor of the Harvest Ministry Papua New Guinea, lived there. Pastor Isaiah had been trained as a minister in the United Church. He had decided to start his own Bible college to train missionaries after working with some Fijians working for Every Home for Christ in Bougainville, one of whom was Pastor Josua. Pastor Isaiah was frustrated by the lack of support for mission from the United Church and so decided to start his own church. But, after discovering that his mission statement was very similar to that of the Harvest Ministry, he elected to join the Harvest Ministry instead. Pastor Isaiah had become acquainted with Pastor Vili and other founding members of the Harvest Ministry while living in Suva to attend theological college; he had attended the Harvest Ministry because it was one of the few churches that offered English services.

Pastor Isaiah was not particularly enthusiastic about having Fijian missionaries in Papua New Guinea. He got along well with some of them but thought many Fijians had 'a cultural inability to humble themselves', which made it difficult for them to live among the people they served. I heard from other Papua New Guineans that many (but not all) of the Fijian missionaries insisted on living in big houses in town, a lifestyle that cut them off from their congregations and cost the church a lot of money. Pastor Isaiah said that he had several times had to tell Fijian missionaries that they would have to find housing their congregations could pay for. He told me that Fijian missionaries had been 'part of the deal', which included more desirable things such as places for Papua New Guinean missionaries in East Africa and training for many young Papua New Guineans in Fiji, although Pastor Isaiah also had his own Bible colleges, the largest being outside Lae in Morobe Province of Papua New Guinea, and there were others in Bougainville. Several of the Fijian missionaries who had been posted in Papua New Guinea had been called back to Suva some months before I visited in 2012 and only a couple had been replaced by new Fijian missionaries.

Faithfulness in Small Things

Visits to Fijian missionaries in Port Moresby, Manus and Lae confirmed that Fijians had no special ability to attract New Guineans to the church. Fijian missionaries had moved from seeing themselves as spiritual guides to Papua New Guineans to seeing themselves as helping disenfranchised youth as fellow 'Pacific Islanders' whose status as outsiders in Papua New Guinea helped them to see things in wider perspective. The Port Moresby branch of the Papua New Guinea Harvest Ministry was the one that most resembled the Fijian church. The Port Moresby church had been strong and vibrant when Pastor Tomasi founded it during his time as a bank manager in the city. But attendance had dwindled under the full-time Fijian pastor who had taken over when Pastor Tomasi returned to Fiji. When I visited in 2012, the church was in the hands of Pastor Jone, a Fijian missionary who had been appointed a few months before to revitalise the church. Pastor Jone told me that he had started out as a schoolteacher but was 'doubly destined' to be pulled into the Harvest Ministry since he was an old secondary school friend of Pastor Vili's and was also married to Pastor Vili's wife's sister. Pastor Jone worked closely in Port Moresby with a group of Papua New Guinean church elders, most of whom were successful urban professionals, some having worked in the bank with Pastor Tomasi.

When I visited Pastor Jone in Port Moresby, he told me that Papua New Guineans could benefit from the advice of Fijian missionaries who had a higher vision and were backed by a strong organisational structure that was necessary to attract people to the church. Pastor Jone laughed about a time many years before when he had been sent to help a church in the Papua New Guinea Highlands and had asked the senior pastor to articulate his vision. Pastor Jone said that the pastor had mumbled something about how Jesus had died for everyone's sins and so now everybody who believed could go to Heaven. 'That was his vision!' he laughed. 'How could his church grow with a vision like that!' Pastor Jone went on to praise the vision of the Harvest Ministry through which young Papua New Guineans could clearly see that if they mastered 'small things', like cleaning the church and conducting music ministries, they would work their way up to Bible college in Fiji and then could go on to preach the gospel to the unreached peoples' groups. He proudly told me of a time when Harvest Ministry pastors had participated in an international conference at which pastors had been asked to articulate their church's vision. The Harvest Ministry had been the only church represented for which everyone had written exactly the same thing because they had a clear vision, a clear foundation of shared beliefs and a clear structure of authority.

Generally, however, Pastor Jone spoke of his Papua New Guinean co-workers and sponsors as equals and fellow 'Pacific peoples'. Successful professional Papua New Guineans occupied the top levels of the church *vanua*, receiving blessings in return for contributing money to help disenfranchised youth to success in church and business. Like Pastor Vili, Pastor Jone spoke of the importance of maintaining a strong community through which the anointing flowed. At the Sunday morning church service, Pastor Jone echoed Pastor Vili (who had spoken on similar themes at the 2012 convention that Pastor Jone and I had just attended) in speaking at length of the importance of having a strong church community where people treated each other with respect. Pacific peoples, Pastor Jone suggested, understood the importance of relationships, both personal relationships between individuals and Jesus, and relationships within the church community. Churches, he suggested, should emulate the first Christian churches described in the Book of Acts, where the disciples and other early Christians all ate and lived together and shared property:

> Now it's important for us to understand that the church program, church activity, is useless if we don't have a relationship … Somebody said the church began in Palestine with relationship; when it went to the Greeks they change it in to philosophy, they philosophised it; when it went to Europe they institutionalised it, with due respect to all the Europeans; when it went to America with due respect to all the Americans—sorry my sister [Karen]—they made it in to an enterprise. But I made my own addition because we are Pacific people. When it came to the Pacific we traditionalised it and currently we are politicising it (laughter. Amen). But if you want strong healthy churches then it's back to relationship. Simple down-to-earth relationship … That anointing will flow wherever you go. So get connected and allow the anointing to affect your life.[1]

---

1   Fijian and Papua New Guinean pastors spoke in a combination of English and Tok Pisin. I recorded and translated sermons and translated Tok Pisin portions to English.

Pastor Jone later explained the importance of relationships to me with an example of a young Fijian couple living in Australia. Their neighbour went through a divorce and lost his house to his ex-wife. The couple, out of kindness, asked him to live with them and become part of their family. Later it turned out that the man got a great deal of money in the divorce settlement through the sale of another property and used it to buy a very large house for himself and the Fijian couple and their children. This just showed, Pastor Jone told me, that you should think first about relationships and caring for other people and then blessings would flow to those who cared. In his sermon and in other conversations with him, it was also clear that, for Pastor Jone, relationships created a strong church community that allowed people to tap into a corporate anointing.

Pastor Jone also emphasised the importance of respecting leaders and submitting to their authority. At a regular weekly prayer session he held for a group of young men working for a Fijian couple, Pastor Jone reminded the young men that one should 'understand the heart, dreams, and lifestyle of the leader, who is the heartbeat of the company. His dreams, vision, and attitude must become yours'. He concluded: 'This business is anointed by God. With or without you this business will prosper. You need to connect yourself.' Pastor Jone went on to tell the young men that, although the Fijian couple who employed them were always friendly and accessible, the young men must understand that they should respect the couple rather than becoming overly familiar.

At a church service, Pastor Jone also emphasised the need to respect leaders. He said that Pastor Vili was a great leader because he was able to 'reproduce his productivity', echoing words I had heard many times over the years in Suva and from American guest speakers. God had told humans, Pastor Jone continued, to 'be fruitful and multiply', and this meant you should not only be productive but also should reproduce your productivity by establishing a clear corporate model that could be reproduced elsewhere and training future leaders to replace you. This, in turn, required having a clear vision, being a role model and then making sure you associated with successful people. Returning to the example of the early church in the Book of Acts, Pastor Jone emphasised that part of honouring and respecting others in a community—an essential part of building and maintaining relationships— was respecting teachers and leaders. In his Suva sermon, Pastor Jone criticised Pastor Vili's children who often just helped themselves to soft drinks from his office refrigerator. One should respect leaders, not take advantage of their kind nature.

Pastor Jone's 'vision', which he articulated on several occasions, was clear: an organisation such as a church or business should have an anointed leader with a strong vision and institutional structure. Successful Papua New Guineans occupied much the same place as successful Fijians in this vision, serving as guides to youth. Others could succeed through loyalty and submission and particularly in what he called 'faithfulness in small things'—that is, doing lower-level jobs for the leader and then working their way up. Pastor Jone introduced me to several young Papua New Guineans who seemed to confirm this idea: they had been taken in by Fijian missionaries or other leaders, had worked faithfully for the church or business performing small tasks, and, after showing their merit, had been sent to Bible school in Fiji for one-year courses. The church had also sponsored Adam, a young Papua New Guinean recruited by Pastor Tomasi, to work with Pastor Inoke and his family in Kenya. In Suva, Ronny, a young man working as a chauffeur for a Papua New Guinean couple in Port Moresby while he completed high school, spoke to me. He said he liked the vision of the Harvest Ministry and that he hoped someday to be a missionary in Japan. If he served faithfully in small ways, he would earn the respect of church elders, could complete high school and, perhaps, go on to Bible school in Fiji and then on to Japan. A young woman had worked as a housekeeper for two different Fijian missionary families and had moved to Fiji with one of them to continue acting as their housekeeper and to attend Bible college there. She then returned to Moresby where she kept house for Pastor Jone and his family but also offered Sunday school lessons in a poor community. Pastor Jone's words in many ways laid out the Fijian Harvest Ministry 'vision' in Papua New Guinea: through submission to authority, young Papua New Guineans from 'broken homes' and urban settlements who lacked education and had limited prospects could become missionaries and pastors and could travel to other areas of the world.

I later interviewed Pastor Tomasi, who had founded the Moresby Harvest Ministry. Pastor Tomasi, who had been greatly loved during his time in Moresby, had a pragmatic view of the appeal of the Harvest Ministry. He said that he thought many young Papua New Guineans joined because they liked to travel and had few other opportunities to do so. He said that if they worked for the church it was easy to get people to sponsor them to go on trips to other areas of Papua New Guinea and also to other nations, something I observed to be true. Pastor Tomasi's interpretation was interesting in that it portrayed Papua New Guineans, world famous for seeking mystical means to wealth in cargo cults, as approaching the church in a pragmatic way to gain access to the wider world. Indeed, many of the young Papua New Guineans working with the church did seem to be primarily interested in opportunities to travel and see new places.

In Lae, a Fijian missionary couple, Pastor Lagi and Mere, also offered young people with limited prospects training to become pastors and missionaries. Pastor Lagi and Mere ran a very small church underneath their house, which was raised on stilts. The couple were living in the house of a church member who was currently living in Port Moresby. They said they often didn't receive any money from the central church so they had decided to plant gardens. Much of their daily activities involved going off to the gardens each day with a small group of local youths who lived with them and received training on how to conduct prayer services. The young Papua New Guineans also practised their skills by travelling to the homes of successful Lae residents to conduct prayer services. Pastor Isaiah later told me that the Lae congregation had been much larger when he had founded it several years before.

Manus: The Higher Vision of the 'Misfit'

Outside of Port Moresby and Lae, I heard little mention of faithfulness in small things, playing one's role in one's church community, corporate anointing or submission to church leaders who would channel anointing to those beneath them. Instead, sermons emphasised submission to God, a focus on spreading God's kingdom in the 'last days' before Christ's return, and the importance of connecting to a central 'vision' that would allow individuals to improve their lives and to gain access to a wider world community. Pastors also spoke more generally of the need to transcend one's particular experiences to gain a wider vision of life in order to see what was needed to help spread God's kingdom and improve humanity.

In Manus, for instance, a Fijian missionary, Pastor Luke, had recently been reassigned to lead the church after first serving in Wewak, in the East Sepik Province. The Manus church was small, consisting primarily of one extended family group that had broken away from the church to which the rest of their village belonged because of a dispute about lineage leadership. One member of this group had heard of the Harvest Ministry from a Fijian with whom he had worked in Port Moresby, and suggested his family found a branch of the church in Manus. Group members seemed less interested in differences between the Harvest Ministry and their former church than they were in establishing autonomy from the rest of the lineage. Pastor Luke preached a doctrine of individual empowerment, urging people to look past their limited horizons to gain a wider view of life, as leaders like Moses had done when they left their own communities and became leaders of different communities. This construction suggested that Fijians were not intrinsically more advanced that Papua New Guineans but, instead, were sometimes able to give guidance because of their insights as outsiders in a new place.

Pastor Luke spoke in one sermon on the topic of 'barrenness' in one's life, suggesting that people often thought of themselves as coming from tiny villages and tiny islands and not being able to accomplish much. But God, he said, had planted within each person the 'DNA' for greatness in some activity:

> You can say, 'I come from the settlement, I come from a tiny village from this family that has no history'. But you are called to do something ... That something can be very insignificant, but that small something can make a difference in the province. Hallelujah? So when you find out what you are good at and what you are fruitful at ... mark it right and reproduce it; do business with it. Hallelujah? I may not be a good banker or businessman but I learned to be a discipler. I learned, uh, to deal ... with human resources to build them up to encourage them, to empower them. Find out what you are good at and multiply it.

Pastor Luke gave an example from his own life of when he had wanted to leave Bible school, seeing little purpose in what he was learning. He had gone to talk to Pastor Anare, who had an administrative position in Suva. Pastor Anare urged Luke to look out the window of his office in the large central church of Harvest Ministry Suva. 'I couldn't see anything but the roof of the church,' he told his Papua New Guinean congregation. 'I didn't know what he was talking about and then all of a sudden I got it.' 'Do you know what it takes to build a church this size?' Pastor Anare asked him and Luke replied: 'It's OK, I get it.' 'It's all about divine discontent,' he told his congregation in Papua New Guinea. 'You need to be able to see things in a higher view to be able to see what is wrong with where you are.' Here Pastor Luke spoke of the vision that had produced the Harvest Ministry's impressive church in Suva, but made it clear that this was just an example of a kind of larger vision, detached from one's own particular situation, that enabled people to progress and become leaders. He went on, for instance, to talk about Mother Teresa as another great leader who was able to experience a 'divine discontent', that is, was able to see that the conditions, in this case extreme poverty, that were normal in her life experience should be changed.

Pastor Luke habitually spoke to his small congregation about the traits of 'us Pacific Islanders', thus stressing the similarity between himself and his congregation. When he spoke about his role as a missionary, he emphasised that his vision came from being outside of his familiar environment. Using the example of Abraham, Pastor Luke explained that God had a way of 'pulling people out' so they became alienated to make them his leaders:

> God has a way of pulling people out, from where they are, from their comfort zone, from their society, even from their family. Praise the Lord! He pulled Abraham out from his people. He said, 'Leave your people. Leave your family. Leave your land and go to a place I will show you.' Amen. Once again God has a way of pulling out people so that they never fit in again … God takes this alienated, this isolated, this in but out … Hallelujah! [The leaders will say], 'I'm not really like them but I'm called to lead them. I don't really fit in with anybody because He drew me out and He has got something to do with my life [that is, God has some purpose for his life]'. Hallelujah. It's this alienation that defines a deliverer, the loneliness of being surrounded by people that you are not really part of.

Pastor Luke continued in the same vein using Moses, who grew up in the palace among the Egyptians but left to become the leader of the enslaved Israelites, as another example of the way that God's chosen leaders were always culturally alienated misfits. Those who were alienated from their fellow humans were better able to follow God's plans unconditionally:

> What I am trying to share this morning is the loneliness of the misfit, the Moses-ness of leadership where you are leading people that you don't know [and they don't know] what you are talking about … Hello! You are leading people that you don't, that don't like you, and at times you don't like them either because of that human nature that is still within us. Amen! You share your vision; they don't understand. They say, 'What the hell in the world [is he talking about]. That thing can't be materialised.' It's hard but in the kingdom of God [we have to do it]. Without faith we cannot please God. In the kingdom of God, it's about faith.

This rather dark message encouraged the congregation that they could transcend their circumstances by pointing out that a 'misfit' leader might have a higher vision. More directly, however, it implied that Papua New

Guineans would benefit from submitting to the direction of Fijian missionaries, not because Fijians were more spiritually advanced, but because, coming from elsewhere, they could see beyond local ways of doing things. In fact, Pastor Luke delivered his sermon to chastise his congregation for ignoring his directions and failing to show up the previous day when he had asked them to repair the church roof.

Papua New Guineans in the Harvest Ministry: Humility and Connection

By far the most vibrant Harvest Ministry church in Papua New Guinea was under the direction of Pastor Isaiah in Bougainville. Pastor Isaiah ran a Bible college where he trained local youths to run 'combat teams' in more remote areas of Papua New Guinea and had another smaller Bible college further south in Bougainville. Pastor Isaiah was frustrated by some of the Fijians in the Harvest Ministry saying that they were 'culturally' unable to humble themselves and live with the people they served. He implicitly critiqued the Fijian style of leadership when he instructed his own students in early morning training sessions, emphasising that leaders should be humble:

> You are not a powerful minister, you are not a powerful pastor, just because you can wear a necktie and things that distinguish you as a powerful leader, no. It is the lifestyle that you live that can distinguish you. Hallelujah. What sort of clothes Jesus was wearing? Was he recognised because of the clothes that he wore? He lived in simplicity and he was accessible. Even sinners were making their way to him. Hallelujah! He was not high up there so that people would find it difficult to go and reach him. He was here so people could make their way, even touch him. Even the sinners touched him. I want you to write this down. This is an important heading. You should not copy the style of leadership today. Copy the leadership of Jesus Christ. Amen. Put that with this powerful statement: do nothing out of selfish ambition and vein conceit but in what? (humility) Humility considering who? (others as better than yourself) others as better than yourself. Can you do that? A proud man cannot do what I tell you. When you have a selfish ambition in you, you do this: 'Everyone look at me! To get a name I'm going to do that.' That's selfish ambition. But when you recognise the effort of others, 'That brother is much better than me; he is doing something greater than myself'. See this is an attitude you must have. Praise the Lord!

Papua New Guinean Harvest Ministry sermons, prayer meetings and Bible classes placed little emphasis on personal prosperity and focused primarily on cultivating the personal discipline necessary to spread the gospel. Pastor Isaiah, for instance, rose along with the Bible school and combat squad students at three o'clock every morning for an hour of personal prayer. He then met with the students for another hour of 'corporate devotion' between four and five in the morning. His message to the students generally stressed the importance of self-denial, personal discipline and humbling oneself in order to develop a personal connection with Jesus. He pointed out to the students that he himself lived in a humble house made of bush materials and had turned down offers from Australian pastors who also contributed to his ministry to buy him a car, asking instead for a sawmill to help build churches, aid posts and classrooms. He exhorted students not to be concerned with lifting up their own names but instead to think always of serving others; the needs of others should always come first. They must learn self-denial in the form of the ability to go without food, sleep anywhere and live a life of poverty in order to serve others. They should not be tourists always taking pictures of people wherever they went but should aim to make a difference in people's lives by spreading the gospel and building schools and aid posts. Like Pastor Vili, Pastor Isaiah stressed that he was respected in other areas of the world and was treated as an important person in Australia. But he suggested that this respect had been garnered by his humble demeanour.

Pastor Isaiah also stressed the importance of rising above one's personal circumstances to have a larger vision. But, as in Pastor Luke's sermon, this higher vision was not attained through attaching oneself to a leader. I heard no talk of corporate anointing or of pastors as conduits for anointing to their local church communities in Bougainville. Pastor Isaiah instructed his students in one early morning prayer session:

> Don't want to be like a chicken low to the ground, limited in your perspective. [You should] want to be like an eagle who sees things from way up high and zeroes its vision in on its prey and concentrates on this. You need to have a vision; you need to work by faith. When you go in the mission field and things seem impossible go to your personal devotion with God. He will give you the strength to soar like an eagle. Then you will be able to keep your mind on your long-term vision: you will see a clinic there, a school there. Remember that God wants us to be like him. Have a compassionate heart. Go to these people who have been neglected by everyone else in the world,

neglected by the government. Give them schools, clinics, clothes. This is why God wants us to do mission. We are to be like Him and we are supposed to have a compassionate heart.

The Papua New Guinean rhetoric, in short, in some ways turned the Fijian model on its head to suggest that humility and willingness to live a materially simple lifestyle were the keys to spreading God's kingdom. These were qualities already possessed by Papua New Guineans, who were used to hardship, to a much greater extent than Fijians.

This was a message that was particularly appealing to young people in Bougainville. The Autonomous Region of Bougainville, a former province of Papua New Guinea, had won semi-autonomous status after a 10-year civil war to win independence from Papua New Guinea. The protracted civil war, combined with a blight affecting cocoa trees, one of the main cash crops, left Bougainville without electricity outside the main urban centres, without mobile phone reception in many areas, with poor roads and with a whole generation who had received minimal education because they had been unable to attend school for long periods during the civil war. Bougainville had moved from being one of the most developed and wealthiest areas of Papua New Guinea to being one of the least developed regions.

The rhetoric of submission to God and serving a world community promised a path to mobility for those whose prospects were otherwise limited. Through disciplined fasting, personal prayer at early hours of the morning and corporate worship before sunrise, young adults could become missionaries who would travel to other areas of the world. One young man who had left Madang Province to join a Harvest Ministry 'combat team' training in Bougainville told me that he knew that he would end up some day in the United States. He had been adopted by an American couple as a boy and had narrowly missed being taken back to the US because he had been away from the village when they left. Now, he could see that, through his work in the Harvest Ministry, he would end up in the US. Another church elder in Bougainville told me several times how much he had enjoyed mission trips to other areas of Papua New Guinea in his youth. It was great, he said, to see different ways of living and to see new things. Submission to God through prayer and fasting, in short, led to playing one's role in a world community, which led, hopefully, to real physical mobility.

In Alotau, where the Harvest Ministry was also very small, I encountered further scepticism about Fijian missionaries, and a different view of the church mission from that promoted in Suva. The Alotau branch of the

Harvest Ministry had been started by a local man who was a successful businessman in Port Moresby and was married to a Fijian woman. This man was also a descendant of Fijian missionaries who had come to the area with the London Missionary Society in the last century. Most of the members in the Milne Bay Harvest Ministry were closely related to the founding member. Others had been co-workers in Port Moresby. The Fijian missionary who had lived in Alotau with his family from 2004 to 2011 had not been very successful and, by the time he left, the church had dwindled in size to about 40 people, over half of whom were children. According to the annual report the Alotau chairman showed me, this was due to 'lack of commitment and nil visitations from the pastor and his elders'. Pastor Eroni, the Papua New Guinean Harvest Ministry pastor from a nearby island who had been filling in since Pastor Maciu had left, politely suggested that they had preferred to 'localise' the leadership of the Harvest Ministry in Milne Bay because sometimes it was hard for missionaries from overseas to get used to life in Papua New Guinea.

Pastor Eroni started his Sunday sermon by asking the congregation to pray for Pastor Vili. He said that Pastor Vili had set a good example of service to a world community and had a clear vision, but made no mention of Pastor Vili as a conduit for corporate anointing who deserved reverence and submission. In the rest of his sermon, Pastor Eroni spoke of the importance of each individual Christian playing his or her role to spread the gospel to all the people of the earth. He said nothing about the importance of a church community, which is perhaps not surprising given the small size of the local congregation.

Instead of submitting to church leaders and following their earthly vision, Pastor Eroni told his congregation that it was important to submit to God and to fulfil God's vision of spreading the gospel all over the world. He emphasised service to a world community, not a local church community:

> We are created to submit to God: God has purposely created you to become a disciple in every way to submit under the will of God becoming a good disciple in every way … God has created you [for] … ministry. We are to in every way we are to minister to the broken hearted, those who are downtrodden, those who are broken in families, broken in their relationship with others, we are to minister to their lives, restoring their lives back into the family of God, amen praise God, and that's the purpose why God has created us, praise God.

People needed a vision, Pastor Eroni continued, but that vision came from God, not earthly leaders, and was clearly laid out in the Bible as the Great Commission in the Book of Matthew:

> You are responsible and I am responsible for this Great Commission. Hallelujah! Do you believe that the Harvest Ministry mission has impacted change in people's lives, in the lives of the people? Do you believe that? Praise God! So we have to keep this Harvest Ministry vision in its purest form. Hallelujah! Walk out with this vision and work with this vision to bring change into the lives of the people. Hallelujah! The Bible says that without a vision people run wild.

After the service the members of the congregation met with me to discuss the Harvest Ministry. None spoke of the Harvest Ministry vision. Overall, the church's appeal seemed to be the small size of the congregation and its association with particular relatives and friends. One woman volunteered that she had not liked another local Pentecostal church because it was too large and there was a lot of infighting in the congregation and that she liked the personal atmosphere in the small Harvest Ministry congregation where everyone knew everyone else well. Another man volunteered that he liked the Harvest Ministry because it showed you clearly how to achieve 'results' in your life. He paid his tithes and prayed and this had paid off; he had been attacked by a gang of criminals in Port Moresby, but they had let him go uninjured and without stealing his money or passport after finding the Bible he carried in his pocket.

Conclusion

In Suva, Harvest Ministry pastors spoke of Fijians as leaders to whom Papua New Guineans and others were encouraged to submit to gain spiritual enlightenment and economic prosperity. In Papua New Guinea, however, Fijian missionaries portrayed themselves as equal partners of successful professional Papua New Guineans who they joined to offer economic and spiritual growth to youth with limited prospects.

Papua New Guinean church leaders such as Pastor Isaiah also encouraged youth with limited prospects to submit to church leaders. But they more often emphasised that all Christians, leaders and followers alike, should be humble. This reversed the valences of the Fijian rhetoric by suggesting that it was really Papua New Guineans, the humble ones, who were the superior workers in God's kingdom. Papua New Guineans with the Harvest

Ministry complained that sometimes young Papua New Guinean men were sent to work as missionaries under the guidance of a senior Fijian pastor with his family. The Papua New Guineans thought that, in some cases, their missionaries did the work and the Fijians took the credit. Some Papua New Guineans said that sometimes Fijians were unable to humble themselves and thus isolated themselves from the people they served by living in urban areas in middle-class houses. Papua New Guineans implicitly critiqued Fijians when they said that good leaders should not wear fancy clothes and take lots of pictures but instead do real work to transform peoples' lives.

For both groups, the same overarching rhetoric created a sense of agency in a world community. Instead of constructing a new world order where entrepreneurial church leaders constructed distinctive 'brands' through claiming submission from those in their corporations, the Harvest Ministry created a loosely knit network where each regional group seized on the parts of a common rhetoric that enhanced their own sense of agency and connection to a world community.

8

The Power of Networks: Harvest Ministry East Africa

I am riding in the backseat of Josua and Elenoa's SUV on the way back to their home from a regional conference of Harvest Ministry East Africa. I have been in East Africa for only a few weeks, but I have already realised that people tend to significantly underestimate travel times, perhaps to encourage me, and so I am not surprised that after three hours of a trip that everyone assured me would take about four hours, we still seem to have about five hours to go according to the road signs. Josua and Elenoa's lively children have drifted off to sleep, so the couple has taken the opportunity to fill me in on their views of mission. First, Josua tells me, it is important to understand that mission has changed. The old model of missionaries living in remote areas among unreached peoples was impractical. Too much money and time were invested in language training; to live among some remote group and learn their language, he would have to live there for years before he could even begin to spread the gospel, so the return on money invested in him would not be great. Now, he went on, people had learned that they should work through local churches. You recruited and trained pastors from the local groups who already spoke the language, knew the customs and had social networks. These people were well positioned to move into more remote areas to spread the gospel. His role as a missionary, he had learned, was to encourage and motivate people and to supply a vision. I asked what the vision was, and Josua and Elenoa answered simultaneously: 'to spread the gospel to the unreached'.

Josua said that he had learned that his time was best spent if he did not have his own church, since that would tie him down and he would only reach a small number of people. Instead, he spent a lot of time travelling around to various areas of East Africa, speaking at workshops and conferences and trying to keep people motivated. He also worked with various organisations such as Samaritan's Purse, an American group whose Operation Christmas Child program sent Christmas boxes with small gifts and children's introductory Bible pamphlets to non-Christian children. During the period when I visited East Africa, Josua spent a week in Swaziland at an Operation Christmas Child conference, and later helped to run a workshop in the city where he lived. It was not important to build the Harvest Ministry per se, Josua continued, as what church people belonged to was incidental. The important thing was to spread the gospel.

Josua had wanted to go to East Africa long before the Harvest Ministry had decided to send missionaries there. He had worked with Every Home for Christ in Papua New Guinea for five years and had met a man from East Africa there and decided that he wanted to go to this man's country. He and the other 'Fijian boys' working with Every Home had been called back to Fiji and he worked there for a while. When he heard that Pastor Vili was recruiting two couples and two single people to go to East Africa as missionaries he was really excited. He wanted to go so much that he asked Elenoa, who he had been dating, to marry him, saying that he had to be married to go to Africa.

Coming to Tanzania, the couple agreed, had initially been very difficult. When they first arrived, they were greeted with suspicion by church leaders who suggested that Tanzania was well beyond the stage of receiving missionaries and that missionaries were 'just like colonialism'. At first, the bishop they were assigned to work with suspected they were trying to steal his church. Later, when Josua wanted to travel around and work with other organisations, the bishop thought that Josua wanted to jump ship and leave his church altogether.

Josua and Elenoa told me that the Tanzanian bishop was not always willing to help with the project of reaching the unreached because he said it was too expensive and wouldn't generate any money, as the unreached were very poor and couldn't pay much in tithes and offerings. When they first arrived, Josua and Elenoa had trained a group of workers to go out and bring the gospel to the Maasai, the tribal group they were supposed to missionise. It had been difficult to get people to enter their training program since Africans were very poor and expected to be paid for everything they did, again probably a legacy of a colonial history in which missionaries had given them things. The bishop had finally seen that their efforts to reach 'unreached groups' attracted volunteers to the church, and so he had come around. Now he was fully on board.

Josua and Elenoa thought sometimes that Tanzanians focused too much on gaining material wealth through churches. But Josua and Elenoa also understood that the people with whom they worked in Africa were objectively much poorer than most Fijians. 'At home,' Elenoa told me:

> It is easy to organise things because everyone brings food; everyone is willing to put people up in their houses; no one is hungry back in Fiji. But here it is different. They are so poor.

They had also come to appreciate the bishop's strategy of financing the church through using church contacts to start businesses and to buy land for farming.

Josua and Elenoa had quickly learned that to operate effectively one must learn the local language and culture. Until you knew the language you really couldn't understand how people were thinking about things. As well, one should never talk about the way things were done back home or volunteer advice. 'You just wait,' Josua said:

> Eventually when people have problems they will ask what you would do and then you can tell them. I share this advice with all the new missionaries. Sometimes they listen to us, and sometimes they don't! I always tell them, 'If you don't do these things then you will always be frustrated and you will really come to hate the people you are here to serve!'

Now, the couple continued, they were very comfortable in Tanzania. The bishop with whom they worked had come to trust them. Josua now spoke Kiswahili fluently and seemed to prefer to deliver sermons in that language. When I played tapes of Josua speaking Kiswahili to people who didn't know him, they mistook him for a Tanzanian. Josua and Elenoa wanted their children to become citizens of Tanzania. When they went back to Fiji, they no longer fit in. Elenoa volunteered that when they had last gone to a conference in Fiji about five years before, they had shown a video of a church in a remote area in Tanzania. The audience in Fiji had started to laugh and she and Josua couldn't figure out why they were laughing until someone told them that the Fijians thought that one woman standing praying while holding a big pot on top of her head was really funny. They had been a bit offended by the Fijians' reaction, the couple explained, and felt very distant from them.

Josua and Elenoa had embraced their new country. 'We really need to build up our country,' Josua observed, referring to Tanzania:

> We are working now on making the church self-supporting by planting crops for rural pastors. They tend the crop and take part to feed their family and give part to the church to fund expansion or improvements in facilities. People here are used to handouts from missionaries. This is because of colonialism. The British and the French and others used to just give people things and the first missionaries did that too so people expect things from you. But we are low budget missionaries. We don't have much. And besides, you need churches to be self-sufficient because foreign aid is very unreliable.

Pastor Josua's remarks raised many of the key themes of Harvest Ministry East Africa. First, as in Papua New Guinea, there was no automatic connection between Fijians and East Africans as fellow Christians in the global south. Organisations such as Youth with a Mission thought that there would be a natural solidarity between Pacific Islanders and Africans because both were accustomed to a lack of material wealth and because, as 'fellow black skins', as one Papua New Guinean put it, Pacific Islanders would not be associated with the evils of colonialism. But East Africans, the Fijians reported, looked on Fijian missionaries with suspicion, sometimes comparing them to former colonialists, and wondered whether they would be useful since they often couldn't speak the local languages. Fijians were called *muzungu* (foreigner, white skin) by Africans, perhaps because, in the wake of structural adjustment in East Africa, people were eager to cultivate contacts with outsiders with resources and so were more interested in seeing people as potentially wealthy foreigners than as being like themselves.

Fijians, on the other hand, were accustomed to images of childlike, 'primitive' Africans and it took missionaries some time to adjust to a reality in which people had been Christian for a long time, and seemed eager, from the Fijian point of view, to exploit and manipulate foreigners. Some Fijians, like Josua and Elenoa, approached their work with a relativistic attitude and learned to understand and work well with people in East Africa. But this was not always the case and, as a group, I suspect that Fijians did not fit into local cultures any better than Europeans and Americans.

Second, the reactions of Pacific Islanders and East Africans to each other indicated more general problems with the idea of natural solidarity between peoples of the global south, since the colonial and postcolonial conditions that Pacific Islanders and East Africans had experienced were very different, leading to misunderstandings. East Africans had been hit by the International Monetary Fund's and the World Bank's structural adjustment policies, severely limiting the kinds of comfortable government jobs that many educated people of previous generations had taken for granted. East African governments now encouraged international NGOs and churches to fill the gap by providing many basic services, like care for orphans, building schools in remote areas and so on (Bornstein 2005). One strategy for people who could no longer get government-funded jobs was to start their own businesses, churches or NGOs, and such people were often dependent for support on networking with anyone they could, foreign or local. Fijians, who had not experienced structural adjustment back home, were sometimes puzzled by the entrepreneurial drive of their East African counterparts and disapproved of what they took to be an inappropriate desire to use the church to make money. Those like Josua and Elenoa who were able to make it past this initial reaction began to understand the East African point of view, which focused on the importance of forming networks to make connections among equals in the face of a reality that was objectively a great deal more difficult than that typically experienced in Fiji. However, initially, the Fijians and Papua New Guineans I spoke to experienced their East African counterparts as inappropriately using religion to make money.

Third, Fijians and East Africans had different understandings of the prosperity gospel. Relatively comfortable middle-class Fijians in Suva saw themselves as considerably healthier and more prosperous than people from many areas of the world. The Harvest Ministry helped such people turn prosperity into agency by prompting them to identify with Euro-Americans as people who could now share their wealth and wisdom with others. But, like Papua New Guineans, East Africans did not see themselves as in need of guidance from Fijians and instead liked the idea of the transnational Word of Faith movement as a network of equals who could exchange knowledge, expertise and resources, and could band together to increase their political clout. Both Pacific Islanders and East Africans looked to the prosperity gospel to increase their sense of agency at home and in a world community.

Culture Clash

Fijian and Papua New Guinean missionaries generally arrived in Africa with images of remote, 'unreached' peoples who had 'not yet heard their first gospel' and, possibly, had never been exposed to clothes, clean water and Western biomedicine because they lived in remote locations and had been neglected by their own governments and the world community at large. These childlike, simple people were imagined as having a natural spirituality and as being deeply grateful for gifts of clothing, schools and the gospel.

On arrival in Africa, however, Fijians found themselves faced with 'three churches on every corner', as one former missionary put it, and with people who seemed to use religion to extract money from foreigners. In addition, East Africans often seemed dubious about Fijians' ability to contribute, treated them as foreigners and tried to manipulate them.

For instance, Adam, a Papua New Guinean missionary working in a remote area of Kenya, told me that he was discouraged about his work in Kenya. He could understand the East African lingua franca, Kiswahili, to a limited extent and could speak it somewhat less, but only a few people spoke Kiswahili in the town where he was posted, and he couldn't speak the local tribal language at all. He liked the local pastor with whom he worked, and often ate his meals with this man and his family. But during the day the pastor travelled around on his motorbike leaving Adam, who had no transportation, at home. He spent most of his time at home because when he went to visit people they expected him to bring gifts of food, which he could seldom afford. 'I tell them, look I am a black skin just like you,' he told me, holding up his arm and pointing to the skin. 'But they say, "No, you are a *muzungu* [foreigner, usually used for Europeans and North Americans]. You need to give us something."'

Adam felt that Africans were tricky; he thought that they tried to use churches to get money from foreigners by, for instance, collecting a group of children and dressing them in ragged clothes and taking their pictures so as to trick foreign donors into thinking they ran orphanages. This was a story I heard from several people. Adam was also dismayed that local church leaders sometimes did not appreciate the sacrifice the Pacific Islanders were making in coming to Africa. One local bishop, for instance, had threatened to get Pastor Inoke's work permits revoked, saying that they were supposed to be working to build his church, not starting a new competitor church. 'I told him,' Adam relayed to me:

that Pastor Inoke and his family left their own families back in Fiji and came here to help Africans and they shouldn't treat them like that. I said that Pastor Inoke was not working for them because they didn't pay his salary.

Adam's impressions were shared by some of the other Pacific Island missionaries. Pastor Mosese, for instance, asked me if I had noticed that there were three or four churches on every block in East Africa. When I agreed that this was so and asked if perhaps Fijian missionaries were superfluous, he said that Africans had a lot of churches, but they were often run as businesses—ways of attracting foreign donations—so they still needed spiritual guidance. Pastor Levy, another Fijian missionary in East Africa, confessed to me that he and his wife Siteri had been very discouraged for the first couple of years in Africa. They had been sent to work with a local family who had a church that trained workers to spread the gospel in a remote area. Levy and Siteri, however, felt that this endeavour was like a family business where the sons ran around publicising their work in spreading the gospel to attract foreign donations and to bring in people as tourists who booked their trips through the family travel agency. They focused on big showy events, such as bringing in prominent guest speakers, to attract foreign donations and left the workers they recruited to spread the gospel with very little understanding of what they were doing. He also said that the family sometimes mixed 'business and church' in a way that seemed inappropriate, using the church to cultivate business contacts and planting churches in remote areas as a way of getting to know people in these areas who could sell them gold nuggets. Pastor Levy understood that one needed to raise funds, but he and his wife were really more interested in spreading the gospel than doing that sort of thing.

Fijian pastors also found their African congregations to be overly materialistic; in sermons, they tried to convince their audience that, while God rewarded the faithful with prosperity and good health, one should not go to church simply to get material things. For example, Pastor Levy told me that when he and Siteri had first arrived it seemed to them that people in the country they served often went to church just to get money, which they felt was a legacy of the European churches that had been active in the colonial period. They needed to be shown that the true message of the Bible was about how to change their way of life and mindset. This would make them more prosperous; however, they should not do it for that reason but to spread the kingdom of God. When delivering a sermon to a church that had expressed interest in joining the Harvest Ministry, Pastor Levy reminded the congregation that one should seek God's anointing not to get wealth, but to spread God's kingdom on earth in preparation for the imminent return of Christ:

> The only reason why you are filled with the anointing, why you are filled with the spirit of God, why you are filled with the fire of God, is to be a powerful witness of the gospel. Hallelujah! Hallelujah! Hallelujah! Amen, amen? There is no other reason. So many pastors in [East Africa] and Fiji and some other nations, they are using that anointing to get money (laughs). I'm here to tell you, [the] simple reason Jesus said that very first day to his disciples; I want to tell you again today, you want to be a powerful witness of the good news. Hallelujah! (hallelujah) That's why we are here this afternoon. I want to encourage you for this great job ... You have something very important in your heart ... That's what your people are looking for: they are looking for that anointing in your life; they are looking for that answer in your life, Jesus in your life. That is not for your own good hallelujah (hallelujah); that is for the kingdom of God. That is why you are saved, to save others. Hallelujah! (Hallelujah!) Amen! (Amen!)

Pastor Levy emphasised that people should seek God to do His work (not for personal profit) and that, in fact, they were already blessed and should feel confident that they would lead an abundant life. Again, this indicated that Pastor Levy and other Fijians felt that African Christians were inappropriately focused on material wealth. The people with whom they routinely dealt, in urban and less remote rural areas, could be prosperous if they just changed their mindset and realised that they needed to 'work by faith not by sight' to spread God's kingdom to the truly impoverished, remote, 'unreached' peoples who had not yet benefited from the two hands of the gospel.

Changing Views

As Pacific Island missionaries lived in East Africa, they developed more nuanced understandings of Africans, but sometimes retained their ideas about the childlike unreached who would receive the gospel with appreciation. Often the missionaries just concluded that they were stuck dealing with less worthy urban Africans so couldn't spend as much time as they wished with the unreached. This was particularly true of the women, since the Fijian missionaries lived in cities where their children could attend suitable schools and the men travelled to remote areas, leaving their wives and children at home. Siteri and Levy, who had lived in Africa only a few years, were discouraged by the time they spent with urban Africans. Siteri told me that she longed to be able to spend more time with unreached peoples but had to stay in town where they had been posted by their local sponsor. Her husband, Pastor Levy, told me that Siteri sometimes got really discouraged and he had to tell her that this was just the nature of missionary work. You had to work on your relationship with your family and serve as a good example of Christian life to those around you and eventually things would work out.

Similarly, Mereseini and her husband Inoke were often annoyed and even frightened by the behaviour of the people among whom they lived, but they believed that these people were quite different from the unreached peoples who they had come to serve. Mereseini and Inoke lived at some distance from the unreached peoples so that they had access to resources and could try to raise funds from more prosperous urban Africans to serve the unreached. The couple worked through local pastors, to whom they also provided training, to reach the more remote groups. When I accompanied Mereseini on her first trip to visit the unreached peoples the couple had come to serve, she was taken aback by the clusters of signs announcing the many churches and NGOs already working in the area. She clearly understood that the existence of the signs and organisations called into question the idea that these people were unreached and neglected by everyone except Fijians. Pastor Inoke, she said, was always pushing their local contact to go into the most remote areas, beyond the reach of these other organisations, implying that the true unreached must exist in an area even more remote than this rural outpost.

The men in missionary families had more contact with remote groups and developed more nuanced views. Pastor Josua, for instance, took me to visit a Maasai group that had relocated to another area when the grazing pastures in their home region were sold to agribusinesses. Josua had moved past stereotypes of the Maasai as ruled by oppressive elders who prevented progress through witchcraft. He told me that Maasai parents often pulled their young sons out of school to tend the herds of cattle. This was not because they feared witchcraft, but because they didn't see that education led to jobs. However, he also spoke of the gospel helping one group to settle a new area by overpowering witchcraft. But this was not witchcraft from oppressive elders; instead, he said the aggressors were from another group trying to guard their land against incursions by the Maasai.

After many years of working in East Africa, Pastor Josua retained an interest in reaching the unreached, but also spent a significant amount of time trying to make the local churches self-supporting, partly to develop the East African nation where he was posted. He and the East African bishop with whom he worked shared distaste for reliance on foreign aid, which they both described as fickle and unsuitable for long-term planning. They had developed a plan together to help local churches plant crops on their land in order for these churches to use the money to pay their pastors and expand their church buildings. Because they worked together as equals, neither party having significantly greater money or power, the two men, who had initially distrusted each other, had come to a common vision of the future of the church.

Fijian Explanations for Poverty

Fijians were puzzled by the poverty in East Africa since they perceived the natural resources there to be much greater than those of Fiji, where the standard of living was generally better. Despite coming from the global south and sharing a history of colonisation, the Fijian pastors, who generally had only secondary and Bible school education, were less able to critique neoliberalism than many Europeans and Americans. Fijians also had little understanding of the colonial and postcolonial conditions in East Africa, since these experiences had been very different in Fiji where the government was still a major employer and there were still subsidies and tariffs propping up the price of local products like sugar. With limited understanding of global history and economics, Fijians often concluded that Africans suffered from 'poverty thinking' and needed to 'transform their mindset'. I heard from several of them that the legacy of colonialism, where people were accustomed to handouts, had created passivity. All of these views were reinforced by the Euro-American religious organisations they met.

Some of the Pacific Islanders realised that East Africans worked very hard. Siteri, for instance, spoke in glowing terms of her neighbours, who she described as working very hard, rising early in the morning and generally minding their own business instead of gossiping about their other neighbours, as she (and many other Fijians) felt that Fijians were inclined to do. After concluding that East Africans indeed worked hard, Fijians speculated that Africans were unable to 'think big', because they were too bound by the customs of the past. One should 'think big' and escape 'poverty thinking', acting in confidence instead of being limited by one's environment. While messages preached in Suva and in East Africa had similar ideas, they also constructed an implicit world system in which Fijians suggested that they had already long ago escaped 'poverty thinking' and could now pass on an empowered state of mind to others.

A common device was to stress how unlikely it was for missionaries to come from a tiny place like Fiji, implying that if Fijians could accomplish such unexpected things, so could East Africans. For example, in a particularly rousing sermon to an impoverished East African congregation, Pastor Josua spoke of his own beginnings on a small island to emphasise that one should not be confined by one's circumstances:

> Somebody like me, born in a small village very far from town on a small island in the middle of the sea, if you are born there, you think that the only place on earth is your island. Why? Because when you stand on the side of the island and you look to the sea you see the water and the sky they touch each other. And you go on the other side of the island and you look beyond, you see the sky and the water they touch each other. You gonna come to the conclusion there's no other place on earth except my island. Hallelujah? That's how you're gonna think ... But [God] told me, 'Think big'. Hallelujah! If I didn't think big I would never have arrived in [East Africa] because [if I went by what I grew up with I would think,] 'My island's finished I should go home'. From here I will go to Heaven. But when you keep thinking big, one thing gonna change in yourself.

Part of thinking big, Pastor Josua emphasised in another sermon in a different rural East African community, was believing in one's power to give and to make an impact, regardless of one's material circumstances. Pastor Josua teased the congregation for being reluctant to part with their money. God would not want them to give more than they had, he continued; they should be confident that God valued whatever they could give and could do great things with it. He referred to the story of Jesus feeding the masses with just five loaves of bread and two fish. He said that Jesus had originally told his disciple Philip to go and buy food for the masses, but Philip had said he did not have enough money, leaving a small boy, who had appropriate faith, to offer all he had, five loaves and two fish, which proved sufficient to feed the masses. Philip, although he was an apostle, had not understood that whatever he had to offer would be sufficient for God; in contrast, the small boy had had faith that God would value whatever he had to give.

Similarly, Pastor Levy told a congregation in rural Madagascar that success depended on changing one's mindset:

> God is doing a mighty work in this nation; you are a blessed nation. This is a very rich nation … You only see that when your mind is changed … I have heard so many Christians say [this nation] is a very poor nation. That's the wrong word; that's a bad word; that's not Biblical … God has already blessed this nation (amen) amen? (amen) … The very first thing that God created was not Adam and Eve, it was the land. So this land is very blessed land. Tell your neighbour amen (amen!). Receive that message … I came from a very small island; you cannot see it on the map. But I want to tell you today it does not matter where you live. It's very important, your attitude, how you think … Hallelujah (hallelujah) you are a very rich man … You can be a great businessman in this mountain … So start there wherever you are starting, whatever small business you are doing. That is the beginning of a great thing. Amen? (amen) That's the beginning of a great breakthrough in your life. Start small. Hallelujah? (hallelujah) The Bible says, if you are not faithful in the small things, you cannot be faithful in the big things. Hallelujah? (hallelujah) So your small business, whatever you are doing, is a stepping stone to a greater thing.

Later in the same sermon, Pastor Levy again reminded his congregation that their nation was a rich one and called upon them to change their mindset so that they could realise the success that God had planned for them. They should see their personal success as part of God's mission to enlarge his kingdom on earth. The only thing keeping them from the success God had planned for them was a negative mindset and immoral habits:

> We want to see God give us something; we want God to give us a good house, give us a good job but we are sleeping all the time but we are not praying and fasting. We are not doing what God is telling us … God honours those who honour his word. Amen? (amen) … I believe you are hearing something; God loves you; He is starting something; He wants to start in your life (amen) start a new Jerusalem … Enlargement begins in your mindset … Hallelujah (hallelujah) so when you go back today, go and see your small job in God's mentality … It's time to enlarge now; enlarge our vision; enlarge our message; enlarge the way we think. Think the unthinkable … One day you are gonna run a big business … You can change in the way you think and the way you see things.

Similarly, Pastor Inoke and his wife Mereseini felt that the area where they lived in Kenya was rich in resources compared to Fiji and were puzzled by why so many people were so poor. Pastor Inoke seemed to think that people were used to handouts due to colonialism and that they needed to learn to work for themselves. But Mereseini, who had been quicker to learn Kiswahili and to make friends, told me on several occasions that she could see that the people in Africa worked really hard, so she couldn't understand why they were so poor.

Pastor Inoke, in a series of workshops for church workers, frequently reminded his audience that they would be blessed with prosperity but first they needed to undergo a thorough transformation in their attitude to become better servants of the Lord. Pastor Inoke also told his congregation at a Sunday service to raise money for an unreached tribal group, as they were already prosperous compared to that group. He told the congregation that they were blessed with fertile land and plenty of rain so were never short of food. People who complained that they had too many children to feed should see that children themselves were blessings, so they had been blessed abundantly.

These reactions show the limitations of the idea that former colonial subjects from the global south will form a 'natural connection' due to similar experiences of colonialism. Colonialism and postcolonialism were different in Fiji and other Pacific Islands than in East Africa. Further, Fiji, like many other small Pacific Island nations, still received significant foreign aid from various sources and the government was still the major employer, particularly for indigenous Fijians.

Missionaries as Guides

Wherever I travelled in Kenya, Tanzania, Uganda and Madagascar, I heard the same quotation, which my son had also, coincidentally, learned that year in his high school history classes: 'Give a man a fish and you feed him for a day. Teach a man to fish and you feed him for a lifetime.' Fijian missionaries understood it as their purpose to teach men 'to fish' through instilling good life habits and encouraging them to develop appropriate skills, as well as by teaching them to pay their tithes and offerings and develop their personal relationship with God so that God would bless them with health and wealth. There was individual variation, however, in the means through which Fijians promoted 'learning how to fish'. Pastor Inoke was the most committed among the Fijian missionaries to the hierarchical model promoted in Fiji with Fijians transferring knowledge and effecting mindset transformation to East Africans who lagged behind. The other missionaries had more egalitarian views forged through their experiences of working with East Africans.

Pastor Inoke's approach was shaped by the fact that he was partially sponsored by Tukana and Meri, the Fijian couple living in Port Moresby who recruited young Papua New Guinean men to live and work with them, instilling good life habits through such measures as requiring the young men to plant gardens to grow their own food and running a series of mindset transformation workshops. Pastor Inoke, probably under instruction from his sponsors, had followed this model by taking in a group of five young African men and training them in religion through a series of workshops on how to live a good Christian life, as well as modelling such a life by example. A large part of the training Pastor Inoke gave the five young men who lived with his family concerned cooking, cleaning, gardening and good time management; however, he also gave them a great deal of instruction in understanding the Bible, giving sermons, managing a congregation and leading an efficacious Christian life.

This was reminiscent of colonial ideas about transforming the colonised through inculcating what the colonisers perceived as healthy and productive habits in dress, household management, hygiene, cooking, time management and so on (see, for example, Comaroff and Comaroff 1991). This kind of thinking also resonated with Fijian culture. Young people in Fiji, including the children of the Fijians involved in these examples, also did much of the household work. Having your children do the cooking and cleaning was considered good parenting since it trained those who were young and foolish into appropriate ways of behaving. Anointing, like traditional religious agency, flowed when a community was in a proper order, with young people—and people from less developed countries—subordinate to those who were older and wiser.

Pastor Inoke, like his Fijian counterparts in Papua New Guinea, stressed the importance of obedience to earthly leaders and 'faithfulness in small things' in this process of mindset transformation. In a series of workshops for local pastors who wanted to work for the Harvest Ministry and local church workers, he emphasised the concept of a good foundation in one's personal relationship with God. Like other Fijians, Pastor Inoke was disconcerted by what he took to be an overly materialistic approach to the church among

East Africans and stressed that one could not expect to come to church and pray and to be instantly blessed with material prosperity. In particular, he was disturbed by the fact that the young men he had taken in and many of the people in his congregation continually asked him for things. He was also unhappy when he heard that the young men of the household had gotten into the habit of asking to accompany me when I went into town in order to ask me for things during the taxi ride when no one else was around. After a few such incidents, he assembled his church workers for a workshop and told them that if they wanted to prosper, they must first establish a good foundation that involved a thorough going re-examination of their life habits and transformation to a more Godly way of thinking and acting.

At one workshop, Pastor Inoke told his audience:

> We must be spiritually pure like that; get rid of our bad ways. 1st John 1:9 if we confess our sins God will purify us. But we can't just pray and then leave it up to God. We can't just confess our sins and think we are done. We must choose to do the will of the Lord. We must really try to change our mindset. People go to church looking for healing, anointing, promotion in work of God. But there are things in our life that are not right. If you want your ministry, your fellowship, your life to grow put yourself before the Holy Spirit and ask the Holy Spirit to examine you. Reveal all the things in you. You must repent and not just once; repentance is continuous. You must choose to repent. No one will change you; you have to choose to change. So let us choose today to change. Let us choose today to be changed. We usually come to the Lord saying, 'I want this, I want that'. God can help you but God will not release these things unless you change your life.

Pastor Inoke went on to speak of honesty and cultivating one's relationship with God, but as in sermons in Port Moresby and in Suva, the emphasis was on learning those habits through obedience to an earthly leader, himself. He told the young men:

> There are a lot of things that we should leave that are hindering our lives … Let's take the attitude of rebelliousness. Rebellious to the pastor or someone else you are supposed to listen to. If you keep doing it, it accumulates; it destroys you. It detracts you away from where you are supposed to be.

Later, continuing on the same theme, he evoked the hierarchical view typical of urban Fijians, with the senior pastor serving as the conduit for blessings for those who obeyed him. Pastor Inoke spoke of the parable of the wise and foolish virgins, saying that having a good relationship with the Holy Spirit was equivalent to filling one's lamp with oil to be ready for any circumstance:

> Picture this: a pastor who has a good relationship with the Holy Spirit when the senior leader tells him what to do he will do it exactly … The senior leader is operating in the spirit, the junior leaders in the flesh … I can tell when I tell you to do something if you are in the spirit or in the flesh. It took Jesus two years with the disciples. The disciples in the beginning were working in the flesh but when they came into the spirit they did great things. You need to rebuild your relationship with the Holy Spirit.

In his workshops, Pastor Inoke generally emphasised the need to abandon one's culture and to 'go with the flow', by which he meant adopting the culture of the Harvest Ministry—a culture that he portrayed as both Godly and efficacious in practical terms. For instance, in one workshop, he concluded by telling his audience to be on time. Africans, he said, were on 'African time' and if they were supposed to be somewhere at 10 in the morning then they would get out of bed and start preparing their breakfast at about that time and would finally arrive around one in the afternoon. That was why East Africa was so underdeveloped; they needed to develop the habit of being on time. When I pointed out to Mereseini later that Fijians often told similar stories about Fijians living on 'Fiji time', she laughed and admitted that many Fijians were very similar to East Africans. She said that Pastor Inoke must be thinking of Pastor Vili who always emphasised the importance of timeliness.

Other Fijian missionaries were more circumspect but still viewed themselves as teachers and guides. Pastor Josua, after a longer experience of living in East Africa, said it was a bad idea to tell Africans what to do and often spoke of himself as East African, not Fijian. He also spoke of himself as having started with the same kind of attitudes he was recommending that people transcend. But he shared some of Pastor Inoke's views on the East Africans, saying, for instance, that the members of the tribal group he served needed to learn that it was important to educate their children even if there were few jobs, because educated people could start businesses instead of just expecting to get jobs. East Africa, he told me many times, was rich in resources compared to Fiji; people just needed to use them.

Pastor Levy was similar to Pastor Josua in emphasising the need to fit in with the people with whom one worked. As we walked through a national park one day, he joked to me that he would need to learn the cultures of the animals we passed because that was what missionaries did. 'Pastor Vili always tells us, "If you are living with ants, learn to be an ant!"', he laughed. And he was true to his word, working under the leadership of an East African bishop, although he sometimes found this man's practices frustrating. He also, however, felt that the people he worked with were often wrongheaded. He told me, for instance, of a pastor with another Pentecostal church who was unhappy with church politics and wanted to break away. 'I tell him,' Pastor Levy said: 'Don't worry about the church. Just stay home and work on your relationship with your wife. Things will work out.' He explained that one should not get involved in political infighting in churches because God would bless those who led a good Christian life, not those who fought.

Fijians, in short, differed from each other but generally viewed themselves as guides supplying a vision to the Africans they worked with. They perceived Africans as mercenary, partly because they had not experienced the conditions of structural adjustment that made it difficult to survive in East Africa and led to the struggle to piece together networks of support. Educated as pastors, without a larger perspective on world finance or politics, they traced economic success to the spiritual state, a view that was reinforced by many of the European and American Pentecostals they met.

East Africans: The Power of Networks

Just as Fijians and Papua New Guineans took different messages from a common Word of Faith discourse, so it was evident that Fijians and East Africans approached the prosperity gospel differently, and that the world community imagined by East Africans was less hierarchical than that imagined by many Fijians. While some Fijians saw themselves as guides and teachers, East Africans thought in terms of networks among equals where all tried to combine their talents and resources to survive in a challenging world.

The African partners of the Harvest Ministry were polite but sometimes dubious about their Fijian partners. One African pastor wondered what the Fijian missionary assigned to him could do since he did not speak the local language. Others politely pointed out that local churches had already organised missions to remote tribal areas, and, indeed, there was a long tradition of such activity among East African churches. Most of the East African pastors and elders with whom I spoke mentioned that they had gone on short-term missions to tribal groups when they were young. Several people also commented that you did not need to go to remote areas to find unreached peoples—you could find many Muslims and lapsed Christians among your friends and neighbours.

Relationships were strongest among the leaders from various countries who had a common experience of travelling to international conferences. A Tanzanian Pentecostal bishop, for instance, said that he had met Pastor Vili in line in the cafeteria at a Billy Graham crusade in the Netherlands. They had fallen into conversation because Pastor Vili was interested in sending Fijian missionaries to East Africa due to a popular Fijian legend that Fijians had originated at Lake Tanganyika in Tanzania. The bishop told me that he thought this legend must not be true because Fijians were not at all like Africans. Pastor Vili had asked if he could visit Tanzania and the two men had later travelled in Tanzania together to visit some unreached groups. The Tanzanian bishop had agreed to join with the Harvest Ministry, he said, 'because, at that time, we were really struggling and these people had a lot of experience with planting new churches'. He had lost some of his satellite churches when he joined with the Harvest Ministry but overall his church had prospered and he had recruited a group of friends from neighbouring countries who had joined their own church networks with the Harvest Ministry. Another bishop from Uganda said that when he and a group of Africans working with the Harvest Ministry had been brought to Fiji for a conference, he had been struck by the similarities between Africans and Fijians; both lived a very relaxed and friendly kind of life.

East Africans, like Papua New Guineans, imagined a flatter world community of Pentecostals than did Fijians. As in Papua New Guinea, there was less talk than in Fiji of the church community as a vessel of corporate anointing released through obedience to a senior pastor. Instead, people said leaders were important because they had contacts with people overseas who could find resources for local communities (see also Haynes 2017). In the wake of the World Bank's structural adjustment policies in East Africa, many services formerly offered by the government were now obtained through NGOs, many religiously based. In such an environment, a common way of survival was, in fact, to network. People started NGOs and church networks and survived in part by attracting foreign support. Bayart and Ellis (2000) suggest extraversion—that is, creative appropriation of outside resources and sources of power—as a longstanding strategy in

Africa. Englund (2001, 2003) similarly argues that independent Pentecostal churches in Malawi draw on Pentecostal rhetoric, emphasising that all Christians are equal in the eyes of the Lord as a strategy of extraversion, which suggests that wealthy European church members are morally obliged to share their wealth with their African equals. East African bishops working with the Harvest Ministry often talked of the importance of networks to survival and noted this as one of the reasons they had joined forces with the Harvest Ministry.

Bishop Andrew, for instance, was a Kenyan who had left a career in the civil service to establish a network of Pentecostal churches in Uganda and Kenya. When his old friend, the Tanzanian bishop working with the Harvest Ministry, suggested that Bishop Andrew join with the Fijians, Bishop Andrew readily agreed and added Harvest Ministry International onto the name of his churches. Reading between the lines, it seemed that one attraction was the small but regular salary he received from the Harvest Ministry. I visited Bishop Andrew and his family for a couple of weeks in Kampala, Uganda, and later joined him and his team on a crusade to expand the membership of some his churches. Bishop Andrew delivered a series of sermons on the trip about the importance of mindset transformation to success that, at first glance, appeared to have a message similar to that of the Fijians. Closer inspection, however, revealed that the bishop's sermons generally focused on the importance of presenting oneself in ways that would attract support from wealthier people.

At one local church, Bishop Andrew delivered what he described as one of his favourite sermons, saying that people tended to think that God would bless those who were faithful Christians and those who were in need. This, he continued, was clearly untrue since there were many good Christians who lived in dire poverty and had terrible illnesses. One needed, he said, to understand God's principles—namely, that God rewarded those who thought of themselves as winners and acted that way. He contrasted Lazarus, who was content to lie on the ground and eat the scraps that fell from the table of rich people, with Jabez, who asked God for an abundant and prosperous life and received this. Like his Fijian counterparts, Bishop Andrew spoke of the importance of going forth boldly, confident that the Lord would provide an abundant life that transcended one's current circumstances. However, while many Fijians saw mindset transformation as involving obedience to God and to senior pastors, Bishop Andrew emphasised individual confidence:

Now I told you the subject is about the mindset. If we realise how our mindset is and realise that we are not thinking in the line of God, the principles of God. If we don't change, it doesn't matter how much you pray; things will not change. If you think yourself you are poor according to what you have in your pocket, according to what you have around, you think 'I have nothing around; I have nothing in my pockets' and, therefore, you think you are poor. You feel that you are paining; you think yourself that you are sick. If that is what you think then you have a big problem. Now let's come to the story of this man, Lazarus … Lazarus his mindset was he was poor and everybody saw him as poor and every gift he got was the gift of a poor man. There is no beggar who is given 1,000 shillings. They are only given coins because they are beggars.

In another sermon, Bishop Andrew, like his Fijian partners, talked about the importance of associating with successful people and learning their habits, but, again, these habits had less to do with obedience to God and leaders and more to do with individual initiative. In one particularly humorous sermon, he pointed out the fallacy of the old adage that hard work led to success. The hardest working people he knew, he said, were manual labourers who received the least money. His own grandmother had worked hard every day of her life and had ended her life in poverty. Clearly, he said, it wasn't working hard that made one prosperous but knowing the right way to work, which was something one got from associating with successful people and questioning the time-honoured customs handed down from one's parents and grandparents.

Bishop Andrew's message was similar to that of his Fijian partners in many ways; however, closer inspection revealed that much of his advice focused on the power of networking and presenting oneself effectively, in ways that deviated from the views of his Fijian counterparts. When Fijians like Pastor Inoke and Pastor Jone in Papua New Guinea spoke of making connections, they often had in mind connecting oneself to some authoritative elder who one obeyed completely to learn good life habits and tap into his anointing. Bishop Andrew, on the other hand, spoke in terms of individuals learning to cultivate support from rich and successful people by acting like winners. For instance, he concluded his sermon on Lazarus and Jabez by saying that people like Lazarus who acted like beggars would receive only small things from other people. If you thought of yourself as poor and needy you would always be poor and needy. If you wanted to succeed you should act successful. Interestingly, however, acting successful often turned out to be a means of attracting large donations from outside sources who were more likely to give if they thought you had a successful cause:

> The thinking of a beggar when they see somebody who has ability what comes to them is, 'How can he help me'? Even before you have asked that is the mindset. And many people in the church they are beggars. They think the more they talk about their problems the more the rich people will help them because they are poor … In the church in Africa many people believe we are poor because we are in Africa and they always think, 'Who can help us?' If they see a white face like the professor [Karen] here they think at least, 'How can he help us?' That is the mindset of a poor man … But if you feel your mind is set in talking about your problems the more people with money will keep off from you. Nobody wants to be around a person who is talking about problems all the time.

Bishop Andrew also echoed his Fijian partners in talking about how the good Christian and successful person was a giver, not a receiver. But, again, ultimately the message was that giving to *wazungu* (foreigners) could be a good strategy for attracting their support. Bishop Andrew spoke of a time when he had toured the US and everyone had asked him if he was there to go to school or to raise money, because all the Africans they had met in the US were doing one of those two things. 'I told them: "Neither, I am here to preach the word of God",' he said, describing how acting like a winner had ultimately opened doors for him to preach to large congregations in the US. He spoke about how people (like myself) would be happy to support and bless a successful enterprise. If one thought of oneself as a giver, this would in turn attract other people to give to you. He described how he had invited me to come along on a crusade only to find he had no funds for gas. He had not asked me for money, but since he had generously accommodated me in his house on a previous occasion, I had offered him money:

> Karen wanted to join us, I told her … 'You are welcome to come but we are not able to drive our car, we shall come by public means' even by public means we don't have enough money but I did not tell her about the money for the bus … But she said, 'Oh I will be happy; I want to bless your ministry. I am going to buy fuel for the trip'. Praise the Lord! I can give testimonies and testimonies and testimonies where God has seen our needs even without asking. Praise the Lord. We can live like princes and princesses if our mentality is not of a beggar but of a giver. When you have a mentality of a giver, people will give you, they will give you, they will give you.

On another occasion, during the same crusade, Bishop Andrew spoke with his pastors and church workers about the power of networking, explaining why he had joined forces with the Harvest Ministry. Andrew told his church elders that he had joined forces with the Harvest Ministry because networks were important in the contemporary world. Each local church, he argued, had its own strengths, just as each of the churches in the early Christian world described in Paul's letters in the New Testament had its distinctive strength. By banding together and exchanging ideas, all could survive and prosper. Bishop Andrew told a gathering of leaders in his church in Kenya:

> We must get organised. We must show commitment. We must share the vision in oneness. Everybody must own the vision of the church and if everybody owns the vision of the church and everybody becomes faithful, I want to tell you there will be no reason why you are not going to grow daily. The church is going to grow daily. God is going to add to the church. When you speak the word the way it is on the foundation of Jesus Christ … When I look all of you I see a very strong [local] church. Today the nations of the world have known the only way to be strong is to have a wider fellowship. When you are standing here as a [local] church your strength is very little even though you are leading yourself, you have all the powers for yourself, you are very limited but we are also very limited. But when we join, when we join as a bigger body we can cause great impact.

The other East African bishops working with the Harvest Ministry also spoke of the importance of networks where relatively powerless people came together to share resources. The Tanzanian bishop with whom Josua worked said that he had decided to join with the Harvest Ministry because his church had been 'really struggling' and the Fijians had a lot of experience in planting new churches. The bishop with whom Pastor Levy was allied was also trying to get the Pentecostal churches in his country to band together and join the African Evangelical Alliance, a branch of the World Evangelical Alliance. He explained to his fellow pastors that if the Pentecostals of their nation joined together they could lobby the national government on issues of common concern and be a force to be reckoned with.

I also found, however, that East African pastors and bishops spoke in straightforward terms of the need to develop ways of supporting churches through local resources, including regularly getting tithes from congregations to pay the salaries of local bishops instead of expecting them to attract money from foreign contacts, since foreign aid was unreliable. A Tanzanian bishop, for instance, laid out his 10-year plan at a regional conference for his pastors. He urged the pastors to educate themselves, saying that everyone these days had access to Trinity Broadcasting Network and to DVDs of famous international pastors such as Myles Munroe. With such an educated audience, if one didn't know the Bible really well, the congregation would see it. He also told them that they needed to step up the pace of church planting because, with the internet, Facebook and other resources, it was now possible to spread the gospel to all areas of the world, including areas that restricted access to missionaries, so the completion of the Great Commission was within reach and Jesus would soon return. He went on to suggest that they needed to build a plan for local self-sufficiency: the head church could help churches get started by giving them money to buy land and materials to build churches. They could also help them establish farming ventures by helping them plant crops, which local people could tend, using the money to support their local pastor and expand the church. But then they must not ask for help from the bishop; instead, they must pay their 'tithe of tithes'—that is, give 10 per cent of the tithes they collected to the head church—which would support the bishop and other leaders who supplied the vision and helped them expand by providing funds to establish other churches. Foreign aid, this bishop told me, was unreliable and could not be used for sustained projects since money just came in now and then and was generally targeted for particular things.

Conclusion

Pacific Islanders and East Africans had no special rapport. Their encounter was informed by contrasting experiences of colonialism and postcolonialism and they had no special connections as people from the global south. However, over time they came to understand and appreciate each other and both sides came to understand the benefits of networking in scarce environments.

Epilogue

I am yet again in Suva for the summer, once again staying with my longstanding host and friend Siteri and her family. In the evenings, I sit and watch TV and sometimes drink kava with Siteri, her mother, Tai Ana, and other friends and relatives. Siteri herself often politely queries my interest in the church, letting me know that she attended the Harvest Ministry for about a year because some friends from work went there but quickly got tired of all the requests for money. She asks me if I wouldn't rather spend Sunday mornings with her attending a Methodist church downtown that many of her friends prefer. Tai Ana is a staunch Methodist who can barely contain her disapproval of the Harvest Ministry and of her many relatives who belong to it. Tai Ana and another relative, Melea, joke about a member of their extended family who likes to attend the Harvest Ministry English services to show off her sophistication. One time they asked this young woman what had been said in the sermon and she clearly didn't know because her English was so poor that she couldn't understand most of it. Tai Ana says scornfully:

> Once her husband sent her money from overseas and she gave $50 to the church even though she has no money because she was sure she was going to get rich! She's just trying to be a high shot, going to English service, showing she speaks good English but she doesn't even understand the service half the time.

I ask Tai Ana about her brother's widow, who I frequently encounter in church. 'She's now working as an usher,' I comment, 'I see her there all the time.' 'Oh yes,' Tai Ana responds, 'She is a lawyer and had a good job but after my brother died her firm closed and now she is working with the church.' We go on to talk about Tai Ana's nephew, who has a bachelor's degree from an American university and is also a devoted member of the World Harvest Ministry. I comment that I haven't seen him in church lately and Tai Ana explains that he is still devoted to the church but no longer has much time to attend since he is working two jobs to support his growing family.

Tai Ana and many other Fijians disparage those who attend the Harvest Ministry, saying that they are putting on airs and have been duped into believing that giving to the church will make them wealthy. Undoubtedly, there are people who look to the church as a road to wealth. Still others attend because they find the services entertaining and lively. But people attracted by promises of wealth and lively services generally move on after a few years. Those who remain faithful to the church like the way the Harvest Ministry provides a supportive and meaningful community for those who want to craft new kinds of communities and leadership roles that highlight professional achievements. Vinaisi and Sunil, Pastor Tomasi and his family, and many others remain faithful and active members of the Harvest Ministry.

The prosperity gospel promises health and wealth to those who give money to the church, but, for Fijians and their affiliates, a large part of the appeal of the prosperity gospel is the ability to convert wealth into agency. Fijians— who Tomlinson (2009) argues experience a sense of disempowerment in the Methodist Church—experience themselves as powerful agents in a world community when they join the Harvest Ministry. They and their partners in East Africa and Papua New Guinea express pride in the fact that they are equal participants in a world network of prosperity preachers. For Fijians and those who work with them in other areas of the global south, the prosperity gospel is not about individual wealth or agency but about creating new kinds of communities (see also Haynes 2012).

Pentecostalism, Robbins (2007) argues, brings rupture with previous moral systems and ways of defining personhood and society. But, for Fijians, Pentecostalism involves both selective rupture and considerable continuity (Mosko 2010) as it becomes part of local projects shaped by local beliefs and conditions. Successful indigenous Fijian urban professionals want to show their rural relatives that they have a new moral system, one that brings the prestige of membership in a world Christian community. But they still want to be valued within Fiji, since local social networks still determine their access to sociality and to important resources like jobs. The Harvest Ministry and other Pentecostal churches are contexts in which they can contest some aspects of *vanua* ideology while retaining others to show themselves as being spiritual and business vanguards helping to channel God's anointing and financial prosperity to Fiji.

Indeed, one symptom of the considerable continuity between Pentecostal and Methodist moral systems was the fact that many women, people from other ethnic groups and younger Fijians eventually left the church because they were tired of being subordinate to senior males. Within Fiji, the Harvest Ministry challenged the chiefly system in some ways but endorsed many other inequalities, posing a very limited critique of society. Newland (2006, 2011) notes that Pentecostal churches in Fiji often support policies favouring indigenous Fijians over Indo-Fijians, despite claims to universality in outreach. Likewise, the Harvest Ministry and other Pentecostal churches tend to reproduce gender and age hierarchies.

Another symptom of considerable continuity with colonial and postcolonial indigenous society is the fact that the Harvest Ministry reproduced many colonial and neocolonial racial hierarchies. While Pentecostal sermons, like the one described in the introduction, prompt people to see themselves as part of a world community of Christians, everywhere people remain embedded in local communities and use Pentecostal ideas and practices to address their own concerns. As a result, local identities remain strong as each group attempts to renegotiate their roles in local communities. Harvest Ministry congregations in Fiji and elsewhere, for example, were largely part of an attempt to create new roles for local middle-class leaders by suggesting that they were respected members of a world community.

And as I write from Schenectady, I am reminded daily on Facebook of my Harvest Ministry friends who have moved from small villages in Papua New Guinea and Fiji to East Africa out of commitment to serve the world community. Of the missionaries I visited in East Africa, only Pastor Josua and Elenoa remain there. One of the Fijian missionaries tragically died in a small plane accident while another returned to Fiji leaving a local bishop to spread the word. Two new Fijian missionary families have now been posted to East Africa. Similarly, most of the Fijians I visited in Papua New Guinea were called back to Fiji and reassigned to local posts within a few years of my visit, following the church's well-established practice of frequently moving pastors and missionaries to new locations. While some missionaries have been called home, others, including some Papua New Guineans who originally served in Tanzania under Pastor Josua, have been sent to establish new missions in East Africa. Some, like Pastor Josua, have forged deep and meaningful connections in the mission field. Overall, however, for most people, the Harvest Ministry remains a very local project wherever it is located, allowing people to craft new kinds of communities and leadership roles that address the conditions of their lives.

References

Abramson, Bob. 2013. *The Fullness of the Holy Spirit in You—For You—With You*. Phillipsburg, NJ: Alphabet Resources Incorporated.

Anderson, Allan. 2004. *An Introduction to Pentecostalism*. Cambridge: Cambridge University Press.

Anderson, Allan. 2013. *To the Ends of the Earth and Back: Pentecostalism and the Transformation of World Christianity*. New York: Oxford University Press.

Barker, John. 2012. 'Secondary Conversion and the Anthropology of Christianity in Melanesia'. *Archives de Sciences Sociales des Religions* 57 (157): 67–87. doi.org/10.4000/assr.23633.

Barker, John. 2014. 'The One and the Many: Church-Centered Innovations in a Papua New Guinean Community'. *Current Anthropology* 55 (S10): S172–S181. doi.org/10.1086/678291.

Bayart, Jean-Francois and Stephen Ellis. 2000. 'Africa in the World: A History of Extraversion'. *African Affairs* 99 (395): 217–67. doi.org/10.1093/afraf/99.395.217.

Becker, Anne. 1996. *Body, Self and Society: The View from Fiji*. Philadelphia: University of Pennsylvania Press. doi.org/10.9783/9780812290240.

Besnier, Niko. 2009. 'Modernity, Cosmopolitanism, and the Emergence of Middle Classes in Tonga'. *The Contemporary Pacific* 21: 215–62. doi.org/10.1353/cp.0.0066.

Bielo, James. 2009. *Words upon the Word: An Ethnography of Evangelical Bible Study*. New York: New York University Press. www.jstor.org/stable/j.ctt9qfgt7.

Boddy, Janice. 1998. 'Afterword: Embodying Ethnography'. In *Bodies and Persons: Comparative Perspectives from Africa and Melanesia*, edited by Michael Lambek and Andrew Strathern, 252–73. New York: Cambridge University Press. doi.org/10.1017/cbo9780511802782.012.

Bornstein, Erica. 2005. *The Spirit of Development: Protestant NGOs, Morality, and Economics in Zimbabwe.* Palo Alto: Stanford University Press.

Bourdieu, Pierre. 1986. *Distinction.* Milton Park: Routledge.

Bowler, Kate. 2013. *Blessed: A History of the American Prosperity Gospel.* New York: Oxford University Press. doi.org/10.1093/acprof:oso/9780199827695.001.0001.

Brison, Karen J. 1999. 'Hierarchy in the World of Fijian Children'. *Ethnology* 38 (2): 97–119. doi.org/10.2307/3773978.

Brison, Karen J. 2003. 'Imagining Modernity in Rural Fiji'. *Ethnology* 42 (4): 335–48. doi.org/10.2307/3773833.

Brison, Karen J. 2007a. *Our Wealth Is Loving Each Other: Self and Society in Fiji.* Lanham: Lexington Books.

Brison, Karen J. 2007b. 'The Empire Strikes Back: Pentecostalism in Fiji'. *Ethnology* 46 (1): 21–39.

Brison, Karen J. 2012. 'Fijian and Papua New Guinean Missionaries in Global Pentecostal Networks'. *Ethnology* 51: 93–109.

Brison, Karen J. 2014. *Children, Social Class and Education: Shifting Identities in Fiji.* London: Palgrave MacMillan.

Brison, Karen J. 2017a. 'The Power of Submission: Self and Community in Fijian Pentecostal Discourse'. *American Ethnologist* 44 (4): 657–69. doi.org/10.1111/amet.12564.

Brison, Karen J. 2017b. 'Kingdom Culture? Transnational Word of Faith Networks' *Social Sciences and Missions* 30 (1–2): 143–62. doi.org/10.1163/18748945-03001002.

Brouwer, Steve, Paul Gifford and Susan D. Rose. 1996. *Exporting the American Gospel: Global Christian Fundamentalism.* London: Routledge.

Burdick, John. 1993. *Looking for God in Brazil.* Berkeley: University of California Press.

Cannell, Fenella. 2006. 'Introduction: The Anthropology of Christianity'. In *The Anthropology of Christianity*, edited by Fenella Cannell, 1–50. Durham: Duke University. doi.org/10.1215/9780822388159-001.

Chesnut, R. Andrew. 1996. *Born Again in Brazil: The Pentecostal Boom and the Pathogens of Poverty.* New Brunswick: Rutgers University Press. doi.org/10.1086/ahr/104.5.1723.

Chua, Liana. 2012. 'Conversion, Continuity, and Moral Dilemmas Among Christian Bidayuhs in Malaysian Borneo'. *American Ethnologist* 39 (3): 511–26. doi.org/10.1111/j.1548-1425.2012.01378.x.

Cohen, Peter F. 2009. 'The Orisha Atlantic: Historicizing the Roots of Global Religion'. In *Transnational Transcendence: Essays on Religion and Globalization*, edited by T. Csordas, 205–30. Berkeley: University of California Press. doi.org/10.2307/j.ctv11hprt5.12.

Coleman, Simon. 2000. *The Globalisation of Charismatic Christianity*. Cambridge: Cambridge University Press. doi.org/10.1017/CBO9780511488221.

Coleman, Simon. 2004. 'The Charismatic Gift'. *The Journal of the Royal Anthropological Institute* 10 (2): 421–42. doi.org/10.1111/j.1467-9655.2004.00196.x.

Coleman, Simon. 2006. 'Materializing the Self: Words and Gifts in the Construction of Charismatic Protestant Identity'. In *The Anthropology of Christianity*, edited by Fenella Cannell, 163–84. Durham: Duke University Press. doi.org/10.2307/j.ctv1198v5x.9.

Coleman, Simon. 2011a. 'Prosperity Unbound? Debating the "Sacrificial Economy"'. In *The Economics of Religion, Anthropological Approaches (Research in Economic Anthropology) 31*, edited by Lionel Obadiah and Donald Wood, 23–41. Emerald Insight. doi.org/10.1108/s0190-1281(2011)0000031005.

Coleman, Simon. 2011b. 'Negotiating Personhood in African Christianities'. *Journal of Religion in Africa* 41 (3): 243–55. doi.org/10.1163/157006611x592296.

Coleman, Simon. 2013. 'Only (Dis-)Connect: Pentecostal Global Networking as Revelation and Concealment'. *Religions* 4 (3): 367–90. doi.org/10.3390/rel4030367.

Coleman, Simon and Katrin Maier. 2016. 'In, of and Beyond Diaspora? Mapping, Migration, and the Production of Space among Nigerian Pentecostals'. *Diaspora* 19 (1): 9–31. doi.org/10.3138/diaspora.19.1.02.

Comaroff, Jean and John L. Comaroff. 1991. *Of Revelation and Revolution. Volume 1: Christianity, Colonialism and Consciousness in South Africa*. Chicago: University of Chicago Press. doi.org/10.7208/chicago/9780226114477.001.0001.

Comaroff, Jean and John L. Comaroff. 2001. 'Millennial Capitalism: First Thoughts on a Second Coming'. In *Millennial Capitalism and the Culture of Neoliberalism*, edited by Jean Comaroff and John L. Comaroff, 1–56. Durham: Duke University Press. doi.org/10.2307/j.ctv11cw8vz.3.

Comaroff, Jean and John L. Comaroff. 2003. 'Second Comings: Neo-Protestant Ethics and Millennial Capitalism in Africa, and Elsewhere'. In *2000 Years and Beyond: Faith, Identity and the 'Common Era'*, edited by Paul Gifford, David Archard, Trevor A. Hart and Nigel Rapport, 106–26. London: Routledge. doi.org/10.4324/9780203398487-8.

Corten, André and Ruth Marshall-Fratani. 2001. 'Introduction'. In *Between Babel and Pentecost: Transnational Pentecostalism in Africa and Latin America*, edited by André Corten and Ruth Marshall-Fratani, 1–21. Bloomington: Indiana University Press. doi.org/10.4000/lhomme.18733.

Cox, John. 2018. *Fast Money Schemes: Hope and Deception in Papua New Guinea*. Bloomington: Indiana University Press. doi.org/10.2307/j.ctv6mtfjm.

Crivella, M. 1999. *Mutis, Sangomas and Nyangas: Tradition or Witchcraft?* Sao Paulo: UCKG Publications.

Csordas, Thomas. 2009. 'Introduction'. *Transnational Transcendence: Essays on Religion and Globalization*, edited by T. Csordas, 1–30. Berkeley: University of California Press. doi.org/10.2307/j.ctv11hprt5.4.

Daswani, Girish. 2010. 'Transformation and Migration among Members of a Pentecostal Church in Ghana and London'. *Journal of Religion in Africa* 40: 442–74. doi.org/10.1163/157006610x541590.

Daswani, Girish. 2015. *Looking Back, Moving Forward: Transformation and Ethical Practice in the Ghanaian Church of Pentecost*. Toronto: University of Toronto. doi.org/10.3138/9781442619586.

Dickey, Sara. 2016. *Living Class in Urban India*. New Brunswick: Rutgers University Press. doi.org/10.36019/9780813583945.

Eastman, Dick. 1997. *Beyond Imagination: A Simple Plan to Save the World*. Grand Rapids: Fleming H. Revell.

Elisha, Omri. 2011. *Moral Ambitions*. Berkeley: University of California Press.

Englund, Harri. 2001. 'The Quest for Missionaries: Transnationalism and Township Pentecostalism in Malawi'. In *Between Babel and Pentecostal: Transnational Pentecostalism in Africa and Latin America*, edited by A. Corten and R. Marshal-Fratani, 235–55. Bloomington: Indiana University Press. doi.org/10.4000/lhomme.18733.

Englund, Harri. 2003. 'Christian Independency and Global Membership: Pentecostal Extraversions in Malawi'. *Journal of Religion in Africa* 33 (1): 83–111. doi.org/10.1163/157006603765626721.

Erasaari, Matti. 2013. '*We Are the Originals': A Study of Value in Fiji*. Helsinki: Research Series in Anthropology, University of Helsinki.

Erasaari, Matti. 2017. '"Wasting Time" the Veratan Way: Conspicuous Leisure and the Value of Waiting in Fiji'. *HAU, Journal of Ethnographic Theory* 7 (2): 309–29. doi.org/10.14318/hau7.2.029.

Eriksen, Annelin. 2008. *Gender, Christianity and Change in Vanuatu: An Analysis of Social Movements in North Ambrym*. Hampshire: Ashgate.

Eriksen, Annelin, Ruy Llera Blane and Michelle MacCarthy. 2019. *Going to Pentecost: An Experimental Approach to Studies in Pentecostalism*. New York and Oxford: Berghahn Books. doi.org/10.2307/j.ctv9hj8pw.

Ernst, M. 1996. *The Role of Social Change in the Rise and Development of New Religious Movements in Pacific Islands*. Munster: Lit Verlag.

Ernst, M., ed. 2006. *Globalization and the Reshaping of Christianity in the Pacific Islands*. Suva: The Pacific Theological College.

Eves, Richard. 2020. 'The Perils of "Yo-Yo" Thinking: Positioning Culture in Pentecostal Healing'. *The Australian Journal of Anthropology* 31: 139–51. doi.org/10.1111/taja.12363.

Fer, Yannick. 2012. 'Polynesian Protestantism: From Local Church to Evangelical Networks'. *Archives Des Sciences Sociale de Religions* 1: 47–67.

France, Peter. 1969. *The Charter of the Land: Custom and Colonization in Fiji*. Melbourne: Oxford University Press.

Freston, Paul. 2001. 'The Transnationalisation of Brazilian Pentecostalism: The Universal Church of the Kingdom of God'. In *Between Babel and Pentecost: Transnational Pentecostalism in Africa and Latin America*, edited by André Corten and Ruth Marshall-Fratani, 196–215. Bloomington: Indiana University Press. doi.org/10.4000/lhomme.18733.

Freston, Paul. 2005. 'The Universal Church of the Kingdom of God: A Brazilian Church Finds Success in Southern Africa'. *Journal of Religion in Africa* 35: 33–65. doi.org/10.1163/1570066052995816.

Garrett, John. 1982. *To Live Among the Stars: Christian Origins in Oceania*. Geneva and Suva: World Council of Churches in association with the Institute of Pacific Studies, University of the South Pacific. doi.org/10.2307/3166046.

Gershon, Ilana. 2006. 'Converting Meanings and the Meanings of Conversion in Samoan Moral Economies'. In *The Limits of Meaning: Case Studies in the Anthropology of Christianity*, edited by Matthew Engelke and Matt Tomlinson, 147–64. New York: Berghahn. doi.org/10.1177/0308275x07086180.

Gewertz, Deborah B. and Frederick K. Errington. 1999. *Emerging Class in Papua New Guinea: The Telling of Difference*. Cambridge: Cambridge University Press. doi.org/10.1017/CBO9780511606120.

Gooren, Henri. 1999. *Rich among the Poor: Church, Firm and Household among Small-Scale Entrepreneurs in Guatemala City*. Bloomington: Indiana University Press.

Groisman, Alberto. 2009. 'Trajectories, Frontiers and Reparations in the Expansion of Santo Daime to Europe'. In *Transnational Transcendence: Essays on Religion and Globalization*, edited by T. Csordas, 185–204. Berkeley: University of California Press. doi.org/10.2307/j.ctv11hprt5.11.

Handman, Courtney. 2015. *Critical Christianity: Translation and Denominational Conflict in Papua New Guinea*. Berkeley: University of California Press. doi.org/10.1525/california/9780520283756.001.0001.

Hardin, Jessica. 2018. *Faith and the Pursuit of Health: Cardiometabolic Disorders in Samoa*. New Brunswick: Rutgers University Press. doi.org/10.2307/j.ctvs32skn.

Harding, Susan F. 2000. *The Book of Jerry Falwell: Fundamentalist Language and Politics*. Princeton: Princeton University Press. doi.org/10.1515/9780691190464.

Harrison, Milmon F. 2005. *Righteous Riches: The Word of Faith Movement in Contemporary African American Religion*. New York: Oxford University Press. doi.org/10.1093/0195153138.001.0001.

Haynes, Naomi. 2009. 'Pentecostalism and the Morality of Money: Prosperity, Inequality, and Religious Sociality on the Zambian Copperbelt'. *Journal of the Royal Anthropological Institute* 18: 123–39. doi.org/10.1111/j.1467-9655.2011.01734.x.

Haynes, Naomi. 2012. 'On the Potential and Problems of Pentecostal Exchange'. *American Anthropologist* 115 (1): 85–95. doi.org/10.1111/j.1548-1433.2012.01537.x.

Haynes, Naomi. 2017. *Moving by the Spirit: Pentecostal Social Life on the Zambian Copperbelt*. Berkeley: University of California Press. doi.org/10.1525/california/9780520294240.001.0001.

Heelas, Paul and Linda Woodhead. 2005. *The Spiritual Revolution: Why Religion is Giving Way to Spirituality*. London: Blackwell.

Hunt, Steven. 2000. '"Winning Ways": Globalisation and the Impact of the Health and Wealth Gospel'. *Journal of Contemporary Religion* 15 (3): 331–47. doi.org/10.1080/713676038.

Ikeuchi, Suma. 2019. *Jesus Loves Japan: Return Migration and Global Pentecostalism in a Brazilian Diaspora*. Palo Alto: Stanford University Press. doi.org/10.1515/9781503609358.

Jenkins, Philip. 2006. *The New Faces of Christianity: Believing the Bible in the Global South*. New York: Oxford University Press.

Kaplan, Martha. 1995. *Neither Cargo nor Cult*. Durham: Duke University Press. doi.org/10.1515/9780822381914.

Keane, Webb. 2006. 'Epilogue: Anxious Transcendence'. In *The Anthropology of Christianity*, edited by Fenella Cannell, 308–24. Durham: Duke University Press. doi.org/10.2307/j.ctv1198v5x.15.

Keane, Webb. 2007. *Christian Moderns: Freedom and Fetish in the Mission Encounter*. Berkeley: University of California.

Kim, Kirsteen and Andrew Anderson. 2011. 'Introduction'. In *Edinburgh 2010: Mission Today and Tomorrow*, edited by Kirsteen Kim and Andrew Anderson, 3–8. Eugene, Oregon: Wipf and Stock. doi.org/10.2307/j.ctv1ddcqhx.4.

Kim, Rebecca. 2015. *The Spirit Moves West: Korean Missionaries in America*. New York: Oxford University Press. doi.org/10.1093/acprof:oso/9780199942107.001.0001.

Lambek, Michael. 2015. 'What's Love Got to Do with It?' *HAU: Journal of Ethnographic Theory* 5 (1): 395–404. doi.org/10.14318/hau5.1.018.

Lawson, Stephanie. 1996 *Tradition versus Democracy in the South Pacific: Fiji, Tonga, and Western Samoa*. Cambridge: Cambridge University Press. doi.org/10.1017/CBO9780511470165.

Liechty, Mark. 2003. *Suitably Modern: Making Middle-Class Culture in a New Consumer Society*. Princeton: Princeton University Press. doi.org/10.1515/9780691221748.

Lindhardt, Martin. 2009. 'More Than Just Money: The Faith Gospel and Occult Economies in Contemporary Tanzania'. *Nova Religio* 13 (1): 41–67. doi.org/10.1525/nr.2009.13.1.41.

LiPuma, Edward. 1998. 'Modernity and Forms of Personhood in Melanesia'. In *Bodies and Persons: Comparative Perspectives from Africa and Melanesia*, edited by Michael Lambek and Andrew Strathern, 53–79. New York: Cambridge University Press. doi.org/10.1017/cbo9780511802782.003.

Luhrmann, Tanya M. 2012. *When God Talks Back: Understanding the American Evangelical Relationship with God*. New York: Random House. doi.org/10.24260/alalbab.v1i1.16.

Macdonald, Fraser. 2020. 'How to Make Fire: Resonant Rupture Within Melanesian Charismatic Revivalism'. *The Australian Journal of Anthropology* 31 (2): 187–202. doi.org/10.1111/taja.12362.

Macdonald, Fraser and Christiane Falck. 2020. 'Introduction: Positioning Culture within Pacific Christianities'. *The Australian Journal of Anthropology* 31: 123–38. doi.org/10.1111/taja.12365.

Maggio, Rodolfo. 2015. '*Kingdom Tok*: Legends and Prophecies in Honiara, Solomon Islands'. *Oceania* 85 (3): 315–26. doi.org/10.1002/ocea.5098.

Malory, J. Lorand. 2009. 'The Many Who Dance in Me: Afro-Atlantic Ontology and the Problem with Transnationalism'. In *Transnational Transcendence: Essays on Religion and Globalization*, edited by T. Csordas, 231–62. Berkeley: University of California Press. doi.org/10.2307/j.ctv11hprt5.13.

Mangowan, Fiona and Carolyn Schwarz. 2016. 'Introduction: Spiritual Renewal and Beyond in the Australia-Pacific Region'. In *Christianity, Conflict and Renewal in Australia and the Pacific*, edited by Fiona Magowan and Carolyn Schwarz, 1–19. Leiden: Brill. doi.org/10.1163/9789004311459_002.

Marshall-Fratani, Ruth. 1998. 'Mediating the Global and Local in Nigerian Pentecostalism'. *Journal of Religion in Africa* 28 (3): 278–315. doi.org/10.1163/157006698x00035.

Martin, David. 2001. *Pentecostalism: The World Their Parish*. Malden: Blackwell.

Massonnier, Andrés Serralta. 2020. '"Pray Looking North": Change and Continuity of Transnational Umbanda in Uruguay'. In *Global Trajectories of Brazilian Religion: Lusospheres*, edited by Martijn Oosterbaan, Linda van de Kamp and Joana Bahia, 153–68. London: Bloomsbury Academic. doi.org/10.5040/9781350072091.ch-010.

Maxwell, David. 1998. 'Delivered from the Spirit of Poverty?' Pentecostalism, Prosperity and Modernity in Zimbabwe'. *Journal of Religion in Africa* 28 (3): 350–73. doi.org/10.1163/157006698X00053.

McDougall, Debra. 2020. 'Beyond Rupture: Christian Culture in the Pacific'. *The Australian Journal of Anthropology* 31 (2): 203–9. doi.org/10.1111/taja.12364.

Meyer, Birgit. 1999. *Translating the Devil: Religion and Modernity among the Ewe in Ghana*. Trenton: Africa World Press.

Miller, Donald E. and Tetsunao Yamamori. 2007. *Global Pentecostalism: The New Face of Christian Social Engagement*. Berkeley: University of California Press. doi.org/10.1525/9780520940932.

Miyazaki, Hirokazu. 2006. *The Method of Hope: Anthropology, Philosophy, and Fijian Knowledge*. Palo Alto: Stanford University Press. doi.org/10.1086/527675.

Morgain, Rachel. 2015. '"Break Down These Walls": Space, Relations and Hierarchy in Fijian Evangelical Christianity'. *Oceania* 85 (1): 105–18. doi.org/10.1002/ocea.5077.

Mosko, Mark. 2010. 'Partible Penitents: Dividual Personhood and Christian Practice in Melanesia and the West'. *Journal of the Royal Anthropological Institute* 16 (2): 215–40. doi.org/10.1111/j.1467-9655.2010.01618.x.

Mosko, Mark. 2015. 'Unbecoming Individuals: The Partible Character of the Christian Person'. *HAU: Journal of Ethnographic Theory* 5 (1): 361–93. doi.org/10.14318/hau5.1.017.

Nazir-Ali, Michael. 2009. *From Everywhere to Everywhere: A World View of Christian Mission*. Reprinted. Eugene, OR: Wipf and Stock.

Newland, Lynda. 2004. 'Turning the Spirits into Witchcraft: Pentecostalism in Fijian Villages'. *Oceania* 75: 1–18. doi.org/10.1002/j.1834-4461.2004.tb02860.x.

Newland, Lynda. 2006. 'Fiji'. In *Globalisation and the Re-Shaping of Christianity in the Pacific Islands*, edited by Manfred Ernst, 317–89. Suva: Pacific Theological College.

Newland, Lynda. 2010. 'Miracle Workers and Nationhood: Reinhard Bonnke and Benny Hinn in Fiji'. *The Contemporary Pacific* 22 (1): 74–99. doi.org/10.1353/cp.0.0105.

Newland, Lynda. 2011. 'The Role of the Assembly of Churches in Fiji in the 2006 Elections'. In *From Election to Coup in Fiji: The 2006 Campaign and Its Aftermath*, edited by Jon Fraenkel and Stewart Firth, 300–14. Canberra: Asia Pacific Press. doi.org/10.22459/FECF.06.2007.23.

Newland, Lynda. 2012. 'New Methodism and Old: Churches, Police and the State in Fiji, 2008–09'. *The Round Table* 101 (6): 537–55. doi.org/10.1080/003585 33.2012.749094.

O'Neill, Kevin Lewis. 2010. *City of God*. Berkeley: University of California Press.

Oosterbaan, Martijn, Linda van de Kamp and Joana Bahia. 2020. 'Lusospheres: The Globalization of Brazilian Religion'. In *Global Trajectories of Brazilian Religions: Lusospheres*, edited by Martijn Oosterbaan, Linda van de Kamp and Joana Bahia, 1–20. London: Bloomsbury Academic. doi.org/10.5040/978135 0072091.ch-001.

Ortner, Sherry B. 2003. *New Jersey Dreaming: Capital, Culture and the Class of '58*. Durham: Duke University Press. doi.org/10.2307/j.ctv1198tvs.

Pauwels, Simone. 2020. '"I Cannot See the Day They Will Make a New Chief": Historically Created Uncertainties about Sacred, Kingly, Populist and Secular Values in Lau, Fiji'. *Anthropologica* 61: 227–39. doi.org/10.3138/anth.2018-0017.r3.

Piot, Charles. 2010. *Nostalgia for the Future: West Africa after the Cold War*. Chicago: University of Chicago Press. doi.org/10.7208/chicago/9780226669663.001. 0001.

Premawardhana, Devaka. 2012. 'Transformational Tithing: Sacrifice and Reciprocity in a Neo-Pentecostal Church'. *Nova Religio: The Journal of Alternative and Emergent Religions* 15 (4): 85–109. doi.org/10.1525/nr.2012.15.4.85.

Premawardhana, Devaka. 2018. *Faith in Flux: Pentecostalism and Mobility in Rural Mozambique*. Philadelphia: University of Pennsylvania Press. doi.org/10.9783/ 9780812294842.

Pype, Katrien. 2011. 'Confession Cum Deliverance: In/Dividuality of the Subject among Kinshasa's Born-Again Christians'. *Journal of Religion in Africa* 41: 280–310. doi.org/10.1163/157006611x586202.

Ratuva, Steven. 2013. *Politics of Preferential Development: Trans-Global Study of Affirmative Action and Ethnic Conflict in Fiji, Malaysia and South Africa*. Canberra: ANU E Press. doi.org/10.22459/ppd.07.2013.

Reinhardt, Bruno. 2014. 'Soaking in Tapes: The Haptic Voice of Global Pentecostal Pedagogy in Ghana'. *Journal of the Royal Anthropological Institute* 20 (2): 315–36. doi.org/10.1111/1467-9655.12106.

Reinhardt, Bruno. 2015. 'Flowing and Framing: Language Ideology, Circulation and Authority in a Pentecostal Bible School'. *Pragmatics and Society* 6 (2): 261–87. doi.org/10.1075/ps.6.2.06rei.

Rial, Carmen. 2012. 'Banal Religiosity: Brazilian Athletes as New Missionaries of the Neo-Pentecostal Diaspora'. *Vibrant* 9 (2): 130–59. doi.org/10.1590/s1809-43412012000200005.

Robbins, Joel. 2004a. 'The Globalization of Pentecostal and Charismatic Christianity'. *Annual Review of Anthropology* 33: 117–43. doi.org/10.1146/annurev.anthro.32.061002.093421.

Robbins, Joel. 2004b. *Becoming Sinners*. Berkeley: University of California Press.

Robbins, Joel. 2007. 'Continuity Thinking and the Problem of Christian Culture: Belief, Time and the Anthropology of Christianity'. *Current Anthropology* 48 (1): 5–38. doi.org/10.1086/508690.

Robbins, Joel. 2009. 'Pentecostal Networks and the Spirit of Globalization: On the Social Productivity of Ritual Forms'. *Social Analysis* 53 (1): 55–66. doi.org/10.3167/sa.2009.530104.

Robbins, Joel, Bambi B. Schieffelin and Aparecida Vilaça. 2014. 'Evangelical Conversion and the Transformation of the Self in Amazonia and Melanesia: Christianity and the Revival of Anthropological Comparison'. *Comparative Studies in Society and History* 56 (3): 559–90. doi.org/10.1017/s0010417514000255.

Robert, Dana L. 2011. 'Keynote Address'. In *Edinburgh 2010: Mission Today and Tomorrow*, edited by Kirsteen Kim and Andrew Anderson, 56–69. Eugene, Oregon: Wipf and Stock.

Rocha, Cristina. 2013. 'How Religions Travel: Comparing the John of God Movement and a Brazilian Migrant Church'. In *Global Trajectories of Brazilian Religions: Lusospheres*, edited by Martijn Oosterbaan, Linda van de Kamp and Joana Bahia, 23–36. London: Bloomsbury Academic. doi.org/10.5040/9781350072091.ch-002.

Rocha, Cristina. 2017. *John of God: The Globalization of Brazilian Faith Healing*. New York: Oxford University Press. doi.org/10.1093/acprof:oso/9780190466701.001.0001.

Rocha, Cristina. 2020. 'Materiality and Global Spiritual Networks: Old and New Sacred Places and Objects'. *The Australian Journal of Anthropology* 31: 210–23. doi.org/10.1111/taja.12357.

Ryle, Jacqueline. 2005. 'Roots of Land and Church: The Christian State Debate in Fiji'. *International Journal for the Study of the Christian Church* 5: 58–78. doi.org/10.1080/14742250500078071.

Ryle, Jacqueline. 2010. *My God, My Land*. Farnham: Ashgate.

Sanneh, Lamin. 2003. *Whose Religion Is Christianity? The Gospel beyond the West*. 4th ed. New York: Eerdmans.

Schram, Ryan. 2015. 'A Society Divided: Death, Personhood, and Christianity in Auhelawa, Papua New Guinea'. *HAU: Journal of Ethnographic Theory* 5 (1): 317–37. doi.org/10.14318/hau5.1.015.

Schwarz, Carolyn. 2010. 'Carrying the Cross, Caring for Kin: The Everyday Life of Charismatic Christianity in Remote Aboriginal Australia'. *Oceania* 80 (1): 58–77. doi.org/10.1002/j.1834-4461.2010.tb00071.x.

Strathern, Marilyn. 1990. *The Gender of the Gift*. Berkeley: University of California Press.

Thompson, E. P. 1966. *The Making of the English Working Class*. New York: Vintage Press.

Timmer, Jaap. 2012. 'Straightening the Path from the Ends of the Earth: The Deep Sea Canoe Movement in Solomon Islands'. In *Flows of Faith: Religious Reach and Community in Asia and the Pacific*, edited by L. Manderson, W. Smith and M. Tomlinson, 201–14. Netherlands: Springer. doi.org/10.1007/978-94-007-2932-2_12.

Tippett, Alan R. 2014. *The Deep-Sea Canoe: The Story of Third World Missionaries in the South Pacific*. Sydney: William Carey Library.

Tomlinson, Matt. 2009. *In God's Image*. Berkeley: University of California Press.

Tomlinson, Matt. 2010. 'Compelling Replication: Genesis 1:26, John 3:16, and Biblical Politics in Fiji'. *Journal of the Royal Anthropological Institute* 16: 743–60. doi.org/10.1111/j.1467-9655.2010.01651.x.

Tomlinson, Matt. 2013. 'The Generation of the Now: Denominational Politics in Fijian Christianity'. In *Christian Politics in Oceania*, edited by Matt Tomlinson and Debra McDougall, 78–102. New York: Berghahn. doi.org/10.3167/9780857457462.

Toren, Christina. 1999. *Mind, Materiality and History: Explorations in Fijian Ethnography*. London and New York: Routledge.

Toren, Christina. 2004. 'Becoming a Christian in Fiji: An Ethnographic Study of Ontogeny'. *The Journal of the Royal Anthropological Institute* 10 (1): 222–40. doi.org/10.1111/j.1467-9655.2004.t01-1-00187_2.x.

Toren, Christina. 2006. 'The Effectiveness of Ritual'. In *The Anthropology of Christianity*, edited by Fenella Cannell, 185–210. Durham: Duke University Press. doi.org/10.1215/9780822388159-007.

Toren, Christina. 2007. 'Sunday Lunch in Fiji: Continuity and Transformation in Ideas of the Household'. *American Anthropologist* 109 (2): 285–95. doi.org/10.1525/aa.2007.109.2.285.

Toren, Christina. 2011. 'The Stuff of Imagination: What We Can Learn from Fijian Children's Ideas about their Lives as Adults'. *Social Analysis* 55 (1): 23–47. doi.org/10.3167/sa.2011.550102.

Trnka, Susanna. 2008. *State of Suffering: Political Violence and Community Survival in Fiji*. Ithaca: Cornell University Press.

van de Kamp, Linda. 2012. 'Afro-Brazilian Pentecostal Re-Formations of Relationships across Two Generations of Mozambican Women'. *Journal of Religion in Africa* 42 (4): 433–52. doi.org/10.1163/15700666-12341240.

van de Kamp, Linda. 2013. 'South–South Transnational Spaces of Conquest: Afro-Brazilian Pentecostalism, Feitiçaria and the Reproductive Domain in Urban Mozambique'. *Exchange* 42: 343–65. doi.org/10.1163/1572543x-12341284.

van de Kamp, Linda. 2016a. 'Introduction: Religious Circulation in Transatlantic Africa'. *African Diaspora* 9: 1–13. doi.org/10.1163/18725465-00901006.

van de Kamp, Linda. 2016b. *Violent Conversion: Brazilian Pentecostalism and Urban Women in Mozambique*. Woodbridge, Suffolk: James Currey.

van de Kamp, Linda and Rijk van Dijk. 2010. 'Pentecostals Moving South–South: Brazilian and Ghanaian Transnationalism in Southern Africa'. In *Religion Crossing Boundaries: Transnational Religious and Social Dynamics in Africa and the New African Diaspora*, edited by Afe Adogame and James Spickard, 123–42. Leiden: EJ Brill. doi.org/10.1163/ej.9789004187306.i-280.42.

van Wyk, Ilana. 2014. *The Universal Church of the Kingdom of God in South Africa: A Church of Strangers*. Cambridge: Cambridge University Press. doi.org/10.1017/CBO9781107298606.

Vasquez, Manuel and Marie F. Marquardt. 2003. *Globalizing the Sacred: Religion across the Americas*. New Brunswick: Rutgers University Press.

Werbner, Richard. 2011. 'The Charismatic Dividual and the Sacred Self'. *Journal of Religion in Africa* 41: 180–205. doi.org/10.1163/157006611x569247.

White, Carmen. 2015. 'Chiefs, Moral Imperatives and the Specter of Class in Fiji'. *Journal of Anthropological Research* 71 (2): 169–94. doi.org/10.3998/jar.0521004.0071.202.

Wiegele, Katharine L. 2004. *Investing in Miracles: El Shaddai and the Transformation of Popular Catholicism in the Philippines*. Honolulu: University of Hawai'i Press. doi.org/10.1515/9780824845759.

Wilkins, Amy C. 2008. '"Happier than Non-Christians": Collective Emotions and Symbolic Boundaries among Evangelical Christians'. *Social Psychology Quarterly* 71 (3): 281–301. doi.org/10.1177/019027250807100308.

Williksen-Bakker, Solrun. 2002. 'Fijian Business—a Bone of Contention. Was It One of the Factors Leading to the Political Crisis of 2000?' *The Australian Journal of Anthropology* 13 (1): 72–87. doi.org/10.1111/j.1835-9310.2002.tb00191.x.

Williksen-Bakker, Solrun. 2004. 'Can a "Silent" Person be a "Business" Person? The Concept of Māduā in Fijian Culture'. *The Australian Journal of Anthropology* 15 (2): 198–212. doi.org/10.1111/j.1835-9310.2004.tb00252.x.

www.ingramcontent.com/pod-product-compliance
Lightning Source LLC
Chambersburg PA
CBHW050844270326
41930CB00020B/3461